The Materials Generator

Renate Vaupetitsch/Nancy Campbell/
Sarah Mercer/Margit Reitbauer/
Jennifer Schumm
(eds.)

The Materials Generator

Designing Innovative Materials
for Advanced Language Production

PETER LANG
Frankfurt am Main · Berlin · Bern · Bruxelles · New York · Oxford · Wien

Bibliographic Information published by the Deutsche Nationalbibliothek
The Deutsche Nationalbibliothek lists this publication in the Deutsche Nationalbibliografie; detailed bibliographic data is available in the internet at <http://www.d-nb.de>.

ISBN 978-3-631-58288-6
© Peter Lang GmbH
Internationaler Verlag der Wissenschaften
Frankfurt am Main 2009
All rights reserved.

All parts of this publication are protected by copyright. Any utilisation outside the strict limits of the copyright law, without the permission of the publisher, is forbidden and liable to prosecution. This applies in particular to reproductions, translations, microfilming, and storage and processing in electronic retrieval systems.

www.peterlang.de

Table of Contents

1. Introduction   7

1.1. The Cognitive Filter: The Interplay between the Mind and the Text
David Newby   11

2. The Art of Writing
Introduction to Section 2   29

2.1. Learner-Generated Criteria for Evaluating Writing
Sarah Mercer and Jennifer Schumm   31

2.2. The ART of Writing: Appropriacy and Register in Text
Sarah Mercer and Jennifer Schumm   37

2.3. Developing an Awareness of the Communicative Nature of Writing
Sarah Mercer and Jennifer Schumm   45

3. Words into Text
Introduction to Section 3   51

3.1. WIT (Words Into Text)
Margit Reitbauer and Renate Vaupetitsch   53

3.2. Grammar Stories: Teaching Notional Grammar through Interactive Story-Telling
Margit Reitbauer und Renate Vaupetitsch   63

3.3. A-I-D-A: From Text Analysis to Context-Sensitive Text Production
Margit Reitbauer and Renate Vaupetitsch   75

4. The EAP of Writing: Enhancing Academic Production
Introduction to Section 4 83

4.1. Creative Use of Source Material
Nancy Campbell 85

4.2. Producing a Synthesis of Academic Sources
Anja Burkert 89

4.3. Improving the Readability of Students' Academic Writing
Nancy Campbell 97

4.4. Writing an Abstract
Ulla Fürstenberg 105

5. Genre Switching
Introduction to Section 5 111

5.1. Using Literature for Genre-Switching
Ingrid Pfandl-Buchegger 113

5.2. Popular Songs: Text in(to) Song – Song in(to) Text
Martina Elicker 125

5.3. Transferring Content across Genres
Sarah Mercer and Jennifer Schumm 141

1. Introduction

What is the aim of this book?

This book is aimed at helping teachers to develop materials appropriate to the needs of advanced language learners at tertiary level. It provides teaching materials, but more importantly suggests ways of generating materials so that teachers can create tasks suited to their specific teaching/learning context. Central to all the ideas is a focus on text- rather than on sentence-level production. The book offers innovative, challenging approaches to working with language at a higher level.

Why is this book necessary?

This book hopes to address the needs of both foreign language learners and teachers at tertiary level:

Learner needs

The target group of learners are those who have already reached B2 level according to the Common European Framework of Reference (CEFR)[1] and are aiming at becoming 'proficient users', in other words attaining C1–C2 level. In order to progress to this level, learners need to develop higher-order textual skills. This means moving away from a focus on sentence level towards refining their understanding of the organisational structures and patterns of longer, more complex texts. Language use at C1–C2 level requires sensitivity to the subtleties of language and to the implications of lexical and grammatical choices on communicative effectiveness. Learners then need to be able to employ this awareness of text

---

1 Council of Europe (2001). *Common European Framework of Reference for Languages: Learning, Teaching, Assessment.* Strasbourg: Council of Europe. This text is also available at: http://www.coe.int/T/DG4/Linguistic/CADRE_EN.asp [accessed 17.12.2008]

characteristics and communicative purposes appropriately in their own text production.

In addition to addressing the linguistic needs of advanced learners at tertiary level, effective teaching materials must also be able to motivate such learners, who have already had extensive experience with the familiar exercises used throughout many teaching books, such as gap-fills and role plays. A fresh, innovative approach to materials design is therefore required in order to offer the learners something different to what they have experienced so far and to help them to maintain their enthusiasm and a sense of progress.

Teacher needs:

Given the diversity of language learning contexts at tertiary level, it can be difficult for teachers to find materials ideally suited to their learners' needs. Some books offer recipe approaches which neglect the individuality of these learning contexts. This book offers a flexible approach to materials design which will enable teachers to generate innovative materials for their specific groups of learners.

How is the book organised?

The book is divided into 5 sections. In the first section (*The Cognitive Filter: The Interplay between the Mind and the Text*), David Newby presents the theoretical principles underlying many of the ideas in this book. The subsequent sections consist of 3 – 4 chapters each. All of the chapters develop different ways of working towards higher-level text production and all have the following structure:

1. Rationale
2. Procedure
3. Example materials
4. Possible variations
5. Annotated bibliography

Section 2 employs some of the key theoretical ideas outlined in Chapter 1 and presents activities aimed at developing learners' awareness of the overall communicative purpose of writing. Particular emphasis is placed on the importance of considering the target readers of texts and on register choice. In section 3, the focus of the activities switches to the communicative purpose of grammar and three innovative approaches are presented which concentrate on the role of grammar and genre awareness in creating effective texts. The chapters in section 4 are all concerned with skill of **mediation**[2] in the writing of academic texts: mediation between source texts and readers as well as between researchers and readers. The chapters in section 5 consider the importance of genre analysis for the production of effective written communication.

Recommended Further Reading

Biggs, J. (1999). *Teaching for Quality Learning at University.* Buckingham: Open University Press.
Carter, R., A. Goddard, D. Reah, K. Sanger & M. Bowring. (1997). *Working with Texts.* London: Routledge.
Cranmer, D. (1996). *Motivating High Level Learners.* Harlow: Longman.
Leaver, B. L. & B. Shekhtman (eds.) (2002). *Developing Professional-Level Language Proficiency.* Cambridge: Cambridge University Press.
Tomlinson, B. (ed.) (1998). *Materials Development in Language Teaching.* Cambridge: Cambridge University Press.

---

2 CEFR (2001: 14) and Newby (present volume)

1.1. The Cognitive Filter: The Interplay between the Mind and the Text

David Newby

1. What does cognitive mean?

The purpose of this introductory chapter is to provide a theoretical background to the ideas and activities presented in this book, which are largely based on a **cognitive approach** to the process of writing. As with cognitive linguistics (see Croft and Cruse 2004; Lee 2001; Robinson 2001), this approach sees both the production and the comprehension of language as a product of cognitive, or mental processes, which are not only responsible for how human beings perceive, categorise and make sense of the world around them but also how they represent these perceptions through language. It follows from this approach that in order to understand language in general, and the process of effective writing in particular, we first need to focus our attention on the human mind and attempt to isolate certain processes which relate directly to language.

In taking a cognitive perspective, we are seeing language, whether spoken or written, as a **process** rather than a **product**. It is therefore not the text itself which is the focus of attention but the processes which give rise to a text. However, emphasising the importance of cognitive processes does not replace the need to examine the nature of texts, which is in fact a prerequisite for text product analysis.

It is customary in language pedagogy to separate skills into so-called **productive** skills (speaking and writing) and **receptive** skills (listening and reading). A merging of receptive and productive skills can be found in the additional skill: **spoken interaction,** which is identified in the *Common European Framework of Reference.* Spoken interaction is defined as instances of language use where "the language user acts alternately as speaker and listener with one or more interlocutors so as to construct conjointly, through the negotiation of meaning following the co-operative principle, conversational discourse". (Council of Europe 2001: 73). In this chapter I shall argue that all language use, whether productive or receptive, needs to be seen in terms of interaction; however, what I mean by this is not interaction in terms of a continuous change from one physical medium of language to another (speaking → listening → speaking etc.) but in terms of the mental interplay that accompanies each separate skill. In the case of writing, this interplay consists of two links: first, between the mind of the writer and the text that is being produced and second, between the mind of the writer and the mind of the reader who is expected to read the text.

A good way to explain the writing process, and indeed any aspect of language, be it grammar, vocabulary or one of the skills, is to represent it in terms of a communication model, as illustrated in figure 1 below. This model has been kept as simple as possible to include only those terms which are relevant here. To produce a model which reflects the true complexity of language processing would of course require a far greater set of categories.

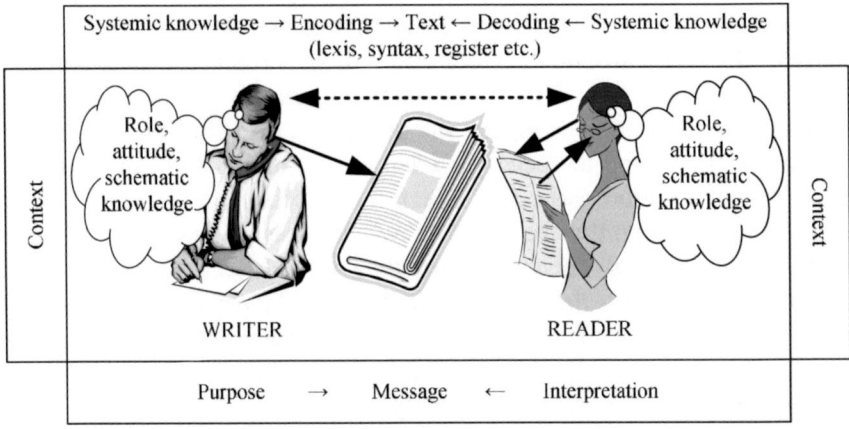

Figure 1: Communication Model: Writing (and Reading)

This model depicts not only the writer but also the reader. The reason for this is that whenever people write a text, they tend to have some image of the reader in their minds. This is indicated by the dotted line between writer and reader. One of the cognitive principles of writing is **reader empathy**, which will be given fuller discussion in section six of this chapter. Thus, it is important to see writing not merely in terms of a text which consists of a fixed set of meanings to be decoded by the reader but rather as an **interactive process** between writer, text and reader.

The *Common European Framework of Reference* (2001: 14) identifies a sixth skill, **mediation**, which is defined as "communication (...) between persons who are unable, for whatever reason, to communicate with each other directly. Translation or interpretation, a paraphrase, summary or record, provides for a third party a (re)formulation of a source text to which this third party does not have direct access." The skill of mediation is central to the writing process and will be addressed in the chapters of this book which deal with academic writing and genre switching.

2. Principles of a cognitive approach

The cognitive approach to writing outlined in this chapter is based on seven general **processing principles** which guide the human mind when writing a text:

- Informativity
- Top-down and bottom-up processing
- Conventionality
- Schematic knowledge
- Reader empathy
- Coherence
- Salience

Whilst the categories will be discussed in a particular order, it should be stressed that this order does not in any way correspond to sequential processing as far as the human mind is concerned. Three points need to be made about these principles:

- processing may be sequential or parallel; for example, top-down and bottom-up processing usually operate in parallel
- the list above does not represent discrete categories; for example, discourse processing and informativity complement each other
- processing is of a cyclical nature; reader empathy will continually be applied throughout the writing process.

3. Informativity

Both within pedagogy and in life in general, human beings make quality judgements about what constitutes a 'good' text. Clearly, the criteria for 'good writing' are not only to some extent subjective but are dependent on the text type in question. Novels such as *Ulysses* are regarded by some literary critics as representing the pinnacle of good writing, yet had James Joyce applied for a job as a writer of manuals for electronic implements, his application would presumably have ended up in the wastepaper basket. Nevertheless, from a cognitive perspective it is necessary to attempt to define what constitutes an **effective** text, one which results in interpretations by the reader that correspond closely to the intentions of the writer. This definition is essentially of a functional nature, reminiscent of types of speech acts identified by Searle (1969). Indeed, it could be reformulated as follows: an effective text is one in which the locutionary content and illocutionary force expressed by the writer through a text are decoded and are in harmony with the perlocutionary effect on the reader. This definition has a cognitive, processing basis but there are of course other criteria of effectiveness. It should be added that the 'effective' criterion applies particularly to what will later be term **unmarked**, conventional texts – letters of application, reports etc. – but less so to **marked** texts, for example, literature in general and poetry in particular. The question of what makes an effective piece of writing is discussed from a text-based perspective by Sarah Mercer and Jennifer Schumm in chapter 2.3. *Developing an Awareness of the Communicative Nature of Writing*.

In order to illustrate how informativity functions it is necessary to focus on the terms 'top-down' and 'bottom-up' processing, which can, on the one hand, refer specifically to language and, on the other, to general knowledge structures. When employing any language skill – writing, speaking, reading or listening – human beings process information in two general ways, which may be thought of in terms of the metaphor 'the wood and the trees'.

Bottom-up processing (looking at the individual trees) refers to focusing on small units of the systemic code (lexis, grammar etc.) and encoding (or decoding) their **sense**, to use a term from linguistics. **Top-down** processing (looking at the wood as a whole, to continue the metaphor) is more concerned with a holistic view of the information to be included in a text: the writer's general purpose or attitude, the conventions accompanying specific text types, the topic, the register and, as far as the language code is concerned, categories which go beyond the level of a sentence.

It should be noted that while writing and reading, language users will make use of *both* types of processing. The distinction is not an 'either-or' distinction; rather these forms of processing work in parallel. As Sarah Mercer and Jennifer Schumm point out in chapter 2.3, when writing a text in a foreign language there is a tendency amongst learners and teachers to focus too much attention on bottom-up processing, which can result in an over-concern with word or sentence level aspects of language to the exclusion of wider aspects of communication. Several of the activities proposed in this book aim to encourage top-down processing.

As the linguist and philosopher, Paul Grice (1975) has pointed out, **informativity** is a basic tenet of human communication. Addressors have ideas, needs, wants etc. which they wish to communicate; addressees assume that utterances and texts they hear or read are meaningful. What Grice terms the **cooperative principle** (ibid.) is at the heart of communication. The question of informativity needs to be considered in light of the bottom-up, top-down distinction. The top line of the communication model of writing in Figure 1 depicts the process systemic knowledge → encoding → code. These terms may be defined as follows:

- **systemic knowledge**: knowledge of grammatical and lexical concepts stored in the mind of the writer
- **encoding:** the process of converting concepts into words and patterning these words into meaningful strings
- **text:** the physical product of this process, i.e. what is read by the reader.

As far as informativity is concerned, we shall consider two types of meaning relevant to further discussion in this book: notional and functional meaning.

a) Notional meaning

Systemic knowledge concerns the storage of concepts in the mental lexicon (i.e. in the mind). The term 'notion', in the sense that it is used in this book, refers to the meaning of a single concept underlying a particular form, be it lexical or grammatical. This definition needs little explanation as far as lexis is concerned: any dictionary lists different meanings of a single form, for example, the word *cup* may refer to the concept or notion of an implement for drinking liquid out of or the notion of a trophy awarded for some kind of achievement. As far as grammar is concerned, a notional approach (see Newby, 1989, 1998, 2003) categorises grammar not in terms of its forms but of the concepts or notions it expresses. A simple definition of a grammatical notion is a single concept underlying a grammatical form.

The four essential principles of notional grammar are (Newby 2008: 34):

- Notions represent the *primary semantico-grammatical unit* of encoding and decoding. Human beings express and comprehend notions.
- Notions are *psycholinguistically real*. They represent concepts stored in the 'mental grammaticon' and utilised in the process of grammaticalisation.
- A notion is an *autonomous semantic concept*. Different notions, even if encoded into the same form, express psychologically separate and distinct grammatical concepts.
- There is a *systematic relationship* between notion and form. A notion is always encoded into the same form.

In the chapter on *Grammar Stories* (3.2.) Margit Reitbauer and Renate Vaupetitsch use the concept of grammatical notions as a basis for story writing.

b) Functional meaning

In Figure 1, the box above the communication model is concerned with code-based concepts which generate meaning or what can be referred to as semantic meaning. The box below the model on the other hand is concerned with a writer's intentions in producing a text or the effect that he or she wishes to produce: that it to say, pragmatic meaning. The role of this type of meaning will vary both in its type and its importance according to the particular text type. For example, the pragmatic meaning of the text you are reading at the moment is of little significance. Basically, all statements are what Searle (1969) terms representative speech acts: i.e. statements of information with occasional illustrative utterances. A text type such as a job application, on the other hand, (see chapter 3.2) will show a wide range of functions.

A functional analysis of language can be applied both from a bottom-up or from a top-down perspective. We may look at the illocutionary force of a **single utterance** or we may look at more general **functional patterns** of a specific **genre**, which Margit Reitbauer and Renate Vaupetitsch refer to in chapter 3.2. as **superstructure**. The development of genre awareness is the focus of section 5 of this book.

4. Conventionality and Creativity

When Mary Shelley, the author of *Frankenstein*, was discussing sending her son to a boarding school, the school headmaster is reported to have said, in an attempt to persuade Mary Shelley of the educational value of his school, "We'll teach him to think for himself", to which she is reported to have replied: "Think for himself? Oh my God, teach him to think like other people!"

This short exchange encapsulates very nicely what, at first sight, seems an apparent contradiction when characterising the nature of language: on the one hand, as Noam Chomsky has repeatedly pointed out, every utterance people make is an act of 'creation'. Creative is a term that is often invoked in connection with writing. Indeed, a common collocation is 'creative writing'. However, it is important to distinguish between 'creative' in a linguistic sense and 'creative' in an artistic or aesthetic sense. To help keep them apart, I shall speak of the former as 'creative with a small c' and the latter as 'Creative with a capital c'. For the writing of many texts types it is only the former that is relevant; in the writing of literary texts both types of creativity will be criteria of their effectiveness.

To consider the exact nature of the linguistic sense of creativity, let us take a definition of language by Bolinger and Sears (1981: 2):

> Human language is a system of vocal-auditory communication, employing conventional signs, composed of arbitrary, patterned sound units and assembled according to set rules.

Two terms in the above definition are relevant to the present discussion: **conventional (signs)** and **set rules**. These indicate that human beings use the same or similar phonological, semantic, syntactic etc. systems when speaking a particular language, otherwise communication would be impossible. In other words, what is referred to in the last section as the 'linguistic code' is conventionalised. For Chomsky and most linguists, creativity refers to nothing more than making use of conventionalised rules in order to 'create' specific utterances, which are infinite in number. The utterances may be novel and appear to be unique acts of creation, but the point is that they are constrained by convention. This conventionalisation also applies beyond the sentence and is relevant to the analysis of the discourse structure of various genres, as Margit Reitbauer and Renate Vaupetitsch point out in their chapters on context-sensitive text production (3.2 and 3.3).

In their chapter on *Learner-Generated Criteria for Evaluating Writing* (2.1), Sarah Mercer and Jennifer Schumm refer to two criteria of conventionality which, according to their students, define effective writing:

- Follows conventions of text type
- Meets reader's expectations

Mary Shelley's riposte: 'teach him to think like other people' reflects the fact that conventionality is a criterion not only for language use but also for cognitive processing and indeed for social behaviour.

In order to ward off the accusation that the aim of chapter 2.1 is to turn learners into an army of language Frankensteins, let us look at the other side of the coin, the creativity aspect of language. First of all, as far as linguistic creativity (with a small c) is concerned, whilst speakers may sometimes use fixed **chunks** of language – *with reference to your email of* ... is one that may occur at the beginning of a business mail – the vast majority of utterances have to be created or 'assembled', to use Bolinger's word, on the basis of rules. In other words, knowledge of the linguistic code – what Chomsky refers to as 'competence' – is the basis of 'performance', the actual use of meaningful language appropriate and relevant to a scenario. It is the skill of 'performing' with language, i.e. creating utterances, that is at the heart of this book and of most language pedagogy. This is reflected in another of the criteria of effective writing cited in chapter 2.1 by Sarah Mercer and Jennifer Schumm: *range of expression*.

A consideration of the second type of Creativity (literary etc.) requires the introduction of an important cognitive distinction: that between marked and unmarked language. Language that is unmarked, be it in the writer's choice of lexis, word order, register, intonation etc., is that which corresponds most closely to the expectations of language users (addressers and addressees) and is therefore most conventionalised. In the case of some text types, it will be the aim of the learner to use largely unmarked language, i.e. that which meets the readers' expectations. At the other end of the scale, one of the criteria for judging the quality of a literary text may well be linked to its examples of marked language, for example, the choice of unusual lexis, the use of unconventional metaphors etc.

Conventionality and creativity are, paradoxical though it may seem, intertwined processes: if we did not know how other people usually think, behave and use language, we would not be able to be creative, i.e. to use language which departs from what we know to be conventional.

5. Schematic meaning

In the thought bubbles of the communicative model of Figure 1, the term **schematic meaning** can be found. This is a general term which, from a cognitive perspective, refers to the fact that words and their denotation or meanings do not consist of discrete units but are part of an interlinked network of both linguistic and general knowledge. The term **mental lexicon** is sometimes used to refer to this wider, cognitive view of language storage. In other words, language use is a **construction** of systemic and schematic knowledge.

What is common to both systemic (linguistic) and schematic (non-linguistic) knowledge is that they are to some degree conventionalised and therefore have the potential to contribute to the construction of meaning. I shall consider three categories of schematic meaning, each of which plays a similar but slightly different role in the transmission and comprehension of messages.

a) Schemata

This kind of knowledge is described by Cook (1989: 69) as "... mental representations of typical situations ... used in discourse processing to predict the contents of the particular situation which the discourse describes." For example, when we read the word 'school', we do not just understand the underlying concept as an isolated entity but in our **mental lexicon** – that is to say, at the back of our minds – there is a pool of knowledge about what a school contains, what happens there, what schools look like etc. This 'pool of knowledge' helps us to make sense of what we are reading. To illustrate the role of **schemata** (singular **schema**) in comprehension, Christine Nuttall gives the following example:

> The bus careered along and ended up in the hedge. Several passengers were hurt. The driver was questioned by the police.

She then says:

> We make connections between the three sentences because we have a schema about buses; this includes the fact that buses carry passengers, and that a bus has a driver. Hence we take it that the passengers mentioned were in the bus and that the driver was the bus driver, not from another vehicle. Yet the sentences do not actually tell us these things: we are making assumptions based on experience. (2000: 6)

Whilst different people may have slightly different schemata for the same word or concept, the fact that schemata are, to a very large extent, relatively conventional structures means that communication can operate fairly efficiently since speakers and listeners share a common pool of knowledge which does not need to be explained or referred to.

b) Frames

Whilst schemata are concerned with concepts stored in the mental lexicon, frames, in the way that I shall define them, are concerned with frameworks of (conventional) context-linked behaviour. This kind of stereotypical situation is known as **frame**, a term deriving from Minsky (1975), which can be seen as a 'remembered framework' or a commonly occurring scenario with which a speaker is familiar. This includes linguistic behaviour. For example, when we receive a holiday postcard from Spain, we expect to read about the sun, the beaches, the nightlife etc. One of the descriptors from the *Common European Framework of Reference* gives a good idea of the concept of a frame:

Uses reasonably accurately a repertoire of frequently used 'routines' and patterns associated with more predictable situations. (CEFR: 29)

Within a cognitive model, frames do, of course, have a non-linguistic counterpart, also referred to in the CEFR:

Social skills: the ability to act in accordance with (the) types of convention (...) and to perform the expected routines, in so far as it is considered appropriate for outsiders and particularly foreigners to do so. (CEFR: 104)

As far as the production of texts is concerned, we might consider a category such as 'text openings'. For example, a personal letter is likely to begin with some kind of phatic proposition 'it's a long time since I've written' etc.; a joke may begin with 'did you hear the one about the man who ...' etc.; a story might begin with setting the scene: 'It was a beautiful day; the sun was shining and the birds were singing ...' etc.

c) Scripts

The third type of schematic structure, introduced by Schank and Abelson (1977), is known as a **script**. This can be defined as an ordered sequencing of thoughts or actions, or a chain of frames. As a cognitive term, scripts can refer to human behaviour in general. If, for example, we think of entering a restaurant, we know from experience that – in the Austrian culture in which I live, but not in Britain – a man goes through the door before a woman; on entering, they find a table; then they are given a menu; then they order the drinks; then they order the food etc. Here we are concerned with behavioural scripts, but this concept can also be applied to language: for example, in teaching speech functions teachers sometimes use cued dialogues based on principles of conversational analysis to show how a greeting might be followed by a reciprocal greeting; an invitation might be followed by an acceptance etc. – so-called **adjacency pairs**. As far as pedagogical grammar is concerned, this takes us into the area of **discourse grammar**. If we wish to teach grammar at discourse level rather than sentence level, then scripts become an important concept. Elsewhere, I have referred to 'meaning chains' or what in a cognitive framework might be termed, **grammatical scripts**. For example in the following dialogue:

A: Have you been to Britain?
B: Yes, I have, I've been to Scotland.
A: What did you do there?
B: I went camping with my parents.

In the first two utterances of the exchange, both speakers express the notions of [Experience]. Then the perspective changes to [Past events], using the past tense. Having identified common grammatical scripts, we can build these into the design of materials and thus provide scaffolding for teaching an important aspect of discourse grammar.

The sequencing of frames into scripts is of particular relevance for the production of texts since scripts go beyond the level of individual propositions or sentences and examine a human being's conventional expectations of how a text will be structured. For example, if we examine many factual texts, we will find that a paragraph may begin with a general statement about a topic before moving on to discuss particular details. As far as spoken interaction is concerned, the *Common European Framework of Reference* refers to "scripts of interactional exchanges" (CEFR: 13). The nature of scripts in written exchanges is considered by Margit Reitbauer and Renate Vaupetitsch in their chapter on *A-I-D-A* (3.3).

6. Reader empathy

The vast majority of texts are written to be read and to some extent are written with a specific reader, or group of readers in the mind's eye of the writer. Exceptions to this are perhaps lockable diaries, tattoos on buttocks. I shall use the term empathy to reflect that fact that when writing, part of a writer's attention is focused on the reader. It should be noted that empathy is not being used in any *emotional* sense but in a *cognitive* sense. There are two important aspects to the question of empathy: the first, of a sociological nature; the second, of a cognitive nature.

a) Role empathy

In their chapter on *Developing Awareness of the Communicative Nature of Writing* (2.3), Sarah Mercer and Jennifer Schumm refer to the receiver and their relationship to the addresser as two aspects of written communication. In the communication model of Figure 1, the categories of writer, reader, role make the same point. From a sociological perspective writers will tend to assess their own role when producing a particular text sort and that of the intended or likely reader. This role ↔ role parameter will have a considerable effect on the register chosen by the writer of a particular text. This register is to a considerable extent conventionalised: with much of human behaviour, including human language, we tend to behave in ways that other members of our speech community do. In chapter 2.1 on *Learner-Generated Criteria for Evaluating Writing* one of the criteria Sarah Mercer and Jennifer Schumm mention is *"Meets reader's expectations"*. For example, the language of this present text is largely formal and the use of an expression such as that used a few lines earlier 'tattoos on buttocks' immediately stands out as what is known in cognitive terms as marked, that is to say, breaking with linguistic (or behavioural) convention. One way of recognising a literary text is by its high degree of markedness.

b) Processing empathy

This aspect of empathy is concerned with the question 'do I think that the reader will be able to understand my text?' Breakdowns in understanding are frequent in both spoken and written communication and can have a variety of causes, some of which may lie within the realms of 'informativity' – using incorrect lexis or notions are obvious examples. In section 7 of this chapter, there is a discussion of breakdowns in coherence. The point that needs to be made is that effective writing requires writers constantly to see their texts through the minds of the readers. Using peer editing in the classroom is one way of developing this ability.

7. Coherence

Various linguists have provided definitions of what constitutes a text, as opposed to a single utterance. Beaugrande and Dressler list seven **standards of textuality** (1981: 3–10), one of which is **coherence**. From a cognitive perspective coherence can be seen as arising from three **processing modes**, all of which are in action when people both write and read texts:

a) a schematic representation, held in the memory and possibly quite vague in nature, of what has already been written about/read in the text – we will term this **past processing**
b) the immediate utterance that is being written or read – **immediate processing**
c) a forward-looking drive which predicts, in very vague terms, what is going to be said and which, if writers are empathetic, might require them to prepare the reader for what is coming and to help him or her to predict certain aspects of the message – **predictive processing**.

Coherence can thus be described as the attempt by writers to keep these three modes of processing in a harmonious relationship, or, as Beaugrande and Dressler put it, "ways in which (…) CONCEPTS and RELATIONS which *underlie* the surface text, are *mutually accessible* and *relevant*" (ibid. 4.). Lack of coherence may cause a breakdown in processing: readers may not understand how one utterance relates to another or how an utterance is relevant in a particular context etc.

There are various ways of maintaining or supporting coherence. One of these is what is often termed linguistic **cohesion:** specific words and phrases (e.g. *however, therefore, last but not least*) indicate the relationship, for example, between past processing and immediate processing, or between immediate processing and predictive processing.

Another way of creating cohesion is **reference** to people, things, actions, facts which have already been written about or will be written about or simply exist in the external world. On many occasions, reference is made grammatically by means of pronouns – *he, she* etc. On others, lexical reference may be used, which will help the reader of a text to recover a referent – i.e. what is being referred to – from his or her memory. For example, I could at this point say 'they wrote their book in 1981'. However, it would be more cooperative and informative to the reader to say 'the authors referred to above wrote their book in 1981'.

A third way of supporting cohesion is what might be called '**orientation**'. This is relevant to the third type of processing, predictive processing, and can be defined as providing information which will help readers to contextualise the utterance that is about to occur or to activate their predictive processing ability. Opening phrases which aid orientation may be conventionalised: *"I am writing to you in connection with ..."*; *"You'll never guess what ..."* etc. Many cohesive devices which occur at the beginning of a sentence have an orientation function: *firstly, to be honest, apparently* etc. These all help to focus the reader's attention in a particular direction – a context, a function, a topic etc. – and prepare the ground for what is to follow.

Finally, it should be added that coherence is a process that is important for both writer and reader. Earlier reference was made to 'reader empathy'. As far as coherence is concerned, maintaining coherence requires writers to see the text they are writing through the readers' eyes and to predict or speculate where they might have difficulties in processing, and to overcome these difficulties.

8. Salience

'Salient' means that something is particularly noticeable or stands out. **Salience** is important in cognitive theory since it recognises the fact that not all information that is encoded into language is of equal importance. Salience will be considered from two of the processing perspectives already discussed: informativity, which will be discussed in terms of **highlighting**, and coherence, which will be discussed in terms of **foregrounding** and **backgrounding**.

As far as informativity is concerned, salience is directly linked to the distinction between marked and unmarked language, referred to above. Highlighting could be defined as the use of marked, or unusual or unexpected language or less conventionalised language. For example, elements of language may be highlighted through use of uncommon lexis or lexical collocations, a switch to inappropriate register, use of creative metaphors or any departures from a reader's expectations of the norm. In phonology, highlighting is often achieved by increased amplitude, marked stress or exaggerated intonation patterns.

However, salience can also be seen from the point of view of discourse and is linked to the concept of coherence. Here we are concerned with what linguists term the **information structure** of utterances. This refers to a writer's option to order or pattern words or phrases in a specific sequence in order to **foreground**, or make more salient, one element of the information and to **background** another. For example, we could write "*I discovered the cat had eaten the goldfish when I got home*" or "*When I got home, I discovered the cat had eaten the goldfish.*" In English, though not in all languages, one underlying processing principle is that of **end focus**; that is to say, the information that comes at the end of an utterance tends to be most prominent. For this reason, it is highly likely that most speakers would choose the second example sentence above. One very common reason for using a passive, rather than an active construction is to provide end focus to certain elements. 'This picture was painted by Klimt' is far more likely to occur than 'Klimt painted this picture'.

Another aspect of information structure concerns the extent to which the elements of information in an utterance are already known or recoverable from a context – linguists often refer to this as 'given', which contrasts with 'new' information. Consider the following options:

a) I first arrived in Austria in 1969. *At that time*, I didn't know that people spoke quite a strong dialect.
b) I first arrived in Austria in 1969. I didn't know that people spoke quite a strong dialect *at that time*.

You will probably agree that a) is more likely to occur. The reason for this is that '*at that time*' refers to 1969, information that has already been processed by the reader. It can therefore be backgrounded by being placed at the beginning of the sentence and therefore given less salience than the new information which comes at the end.

In her chapter on *Improving the Readability of Students' Academic Writing* (4.3), Nancy Campbell considers how awareness of information structure can be developed in writing courses.

9. Conclusion

It is important to take into account all of the cognitive processes mentioned in this chapter in the development of advanced level writing skills, if we are to recognise that writing is not merely a question of applying the linguistic code of English but requires various degrees of processing on the part of both writer and reader. The following chapters present examples of activities which focus on cognitive processes outlined in this introduction.

References

Beaugrande, R. de and W. Dressler (1981). *Introduction to Text Linguistics*. London: Longman.
Bolinger, D. and D.A. Sears (1981). *Aspects of Language*. New York: Harcourt Brace Jovanovich.
Chomsky, N. (1957). *Syntactic Structures*. The Hague Mouton.
Council of Europe (2001). *Common European Framework of Reference for Languages: Learning, teaching, assessment*. Strasbourg: Council of Europe, Modern Languages Division/Cambridge: Cambridge University Press.

Croft, W. and D.A. Cruse, (2004). *Cognitive Linguistics.* Cambridge: Cambridge University Press.

Grice, H.P. (1975). 'Logic and Conversation.' In: P. Cole and J. Morgan (eds.) *Syntax and Semantics 3: Speech Acts.* New York: Academic Press.

Lee, D. (2001). *Cognitive Linguistics. An Introduction.* Oxford: Oxford University Press.

Minsky, M. (1975). 'A framework for representing knowledge'. In: P.H. Winston (ed.), *The Psychology of Computer Vision.* New York: McGraw-Hill.

Newby, D. (1989). 'Towards a Notional Grammar of English'. In: Kettemann, B, et al (eds.) *Englisch als Zweitsprache.* Tübingen: Gunter Narr.

Newby, D. (1998). 'Theory and Practice in Communicative Grammar'. In: R. de Beaugrande, M. Grosman and B. Seidlhofer, (eds.) *Language Policy and Language Education in Emerging Nations, Series: Advances in Discourse Processes Vol. LXIII, pp 151–164.* Stamford, Conneticut: Ablex Publishing Corporation.

Newby, D. (2003). *A Cognitive and Communicative Theory of Pedagogical Grammar.* Habilitationsschrift. Karl-Franzens Universität Graz.

Newby, D. (2008). 'Pedagogical Grammar: A Cognitive and Communicative Approach'. In: W. Delanoy and L, Volkmann (eds.) *Future Perspectives for English Language Teaching.* Heidelberg: Universitätsverlag Winter, 29–44.

Nuttall, C. (1982/2000). *Teaching Reading Skills in a Foreign Language.* London: Heinemann.

Robinson, P. (ed.) (2001). *Cognition and Second Language Instruction.* Cambridge: Cambridge University Press.

Schank, R.C., & R. Abelson (1977). *Scripts, plans, goals, and understanding.* Hillsdale, NJ: Erlbaum

Searle, J.R. (1969). *Speech Acts.* Cambridge: Cambridge University Press

2. The Art of Writing

Introduction to Section 2

The focus of this section is on effective communication in text production. Based on classroom observation, the authors have noted that even advanced learners tend to overlook the communicative purpose of written texts. They often ignore the importance of the appropriate use of register and style, and instead pay closer attention to the grammatical accuracy of their written pieces. This may be due in part to the fact that written texts in the language classroom are generally produced without any interaction with the intended reader, and that traditionally grammatical errors have been weighted more heavily in the evaluation process. For these reasons, the authors of this section propose a series of activities which are aimed at drawing language learners' attention to the range of other elements necessary for effective writing, in particular linguistic appropriacy and communicative purpose.

In the first chapter (*Learner-Generated Criteria for Evaluating Writing*), the authors introduce a flexible, context-sensitive approach to assessment that not only involves language learners in the actual evaluation process but also in the selection of the criteria used. Learners are encouraged to reflect on their own writing experiences and together design an evaluation scheme which is later used in both self- and peer-assessment of specific tasks. In constructing this evaluation scheme, learners become aware of the wide range of factors involved in producing an effective piece of writing for a specific purpose and are able to move beyond a focus on grammatical accuracy. Further, by deconstructing the writing process in this way, learners become better able to monitor and assess their own writing and thus work more autonomously.

The second chapter (*The ART of writing*) addresses issues of appropriacy and register. To help learners better visualize and understand the various degrees of formality used in communication, the authors propose the use of a continuum ranging from very formal to very informal. With the aide of this tool, learners acquire a deeper understanding of and sensitivity to the various degrees of formality. The tool also helps the learner to avoid oversimplifying the issue of register into a dichotomous decision between either formal or informal. The approach suggested in this chapter begins with an analysis of register at the sentence level and proceeds to text production by the learners.

In the final chapter (*Developing an Awareness of the Communicative Nature of Writing*), effective communication stands in the foreground. Learners often focus disproportionately on the linguistic components of written texts, and, in doing so, may overlook the underlying communicative purpose of their writing. In order to help language learners become more aware of this aspect of their writing, a series of activities are proposed. To begin with, learners work through tasks which are intended to sensitise them to the similarities and differences between written and spoken communication. The learners then analyse to what extent a series of different texts are successful in achieving their communicative purposes and provide possible reasons for this. Finally, the learners produce their own texts, bearing in mind the communicative message they wish to convey.

2.1. Learner-Generated Criteria for Evaluating Writing

Sarah Mercer and Jennifer Schumm

1. Rationale

The authors have often observed when teaching writing to adult learners that they tend to overemphasise the importance of syntactical and lexical accuracy in producing effective writing. For this reason, the authors felt it was important to raise students' awareness of other factors involved. The authors have developed an approach to self- and peer-assessment for writing based on learner-generated criteria. Because learners are directly involved in choosing and selecting criteria to evaluate effective writing in their course, they are motivated by their personal investment in the process and gain a deeper understanding of the elements involved in writing at advanced level. Additionally, as the criteria are generated for specific text types and communicative purposes, it is possible to make the criteria sensitive to the particular genre, context and task being worked on by the learners.

2. Procedure

(1) In the first stage, learners share and reflect upon their own personal experiences with text both as readers and writers by responding to a series of questions. (See example materials 1 for possible discussion questions).
(2) After learners have considered their own experiences, feedback and ideas are collected on the board in response to the following question: "What makes an effective piece of writing?" Emphasis should be placed on the perspectives of both the reader and writer. The authors have found a mind-map to be a particularly effective way of gathering feedback. (See example materials 2 for typical types of responses from tertiary level learners in an Austrian context).
(3) Working in small groups and using the ideas brainstormed on the board, learners should choose a set of criteria for evaluating an ef-

fective piece of writing in a particular context focussing on a specific genre or task covered by the class. For illustrative purposes, the genre of film reviews is presented in example materials 4.
(4) Groups report back on their criteria giving reasons for their choices. Together the whole class discusses the results and considers which of these criteria would be most important for writing for this specific task or genre. A vote on the 6 most important is then taken. (6 criteria have been found to be well suited to the authors' teaching context; however, individual teachers may decide upon more or fewer criteria). These are entered on a prepared OHP slide (see example materials 3).
(5) A sample text based on an anonymous former student's piece is then evaluated by the group using the evaluation criteria schema decided on in stage 4. Learners award points to each criteria on a scale of 1 – 10, where 1 = very poor and 10 = excellent. Based on the experiences in using the schema with this text, adaptations and changes can be made by the group as necessary. This stage may be repeated with a range of good/weak examples of student writing. (See example materials 4 for an excellent student text for this genre).
(6) This schema can be used throughout the course by the teacher and by the students in order to peer- and self-assess. Continual use of the schema during the course helps learners to monitor their progress in different areas of their writing. The schema can be re-negotiated throughout the semester as felt necessary by learners and teachers and adapted to specific tasks.

3. Example materials

(1) Possible discussion questions for stage 1:

- What makes a piece of writing pleasurable for you to read in your L1/L2?
- What makes a piece of writing difficult for you to read in your L1/L2?
- In what ways have you found writing in your L2 similar and different to your L1?

- What kind of feedback have you had on your writing in both your L1 & L2?
- Reflect on how you approach reading and writing tasks.
- How do you see the relationship between reading and writing?

(2) Typical responses to the question: "What makes an effective piece of writing?"

- *Good organisation*
- *Follows conventions of text type*
- *Appropriacy of language*
- *Range of expression*
- *Accuracy in spelling & punctuation*
- *Accuracy in grammar*
- *Relevant content*
- *Meets reader's expectations*

(3) OHP slide:

Our 6 Criteria for Writing Effective Film Reviews			
1. *Organisation*	1	5	10
2. *Coherency*	1	5	10
3. *Appropriate content*	1	5	10
4. *Range of expression (esp, film review lang.)*	1	5	10
5. *Appropriacy of style and lang.*	1	5	10
6. *Accuracy*	1	5	10

(4) Example task and student text:

Here is an example of an excellent text written by a high-level learner in response to the task below for a film review[1]. It is included in order to illustrate a text which fulfils the criteria generated by the learners in this context. The underlying rationale behind this flexible approach is that it allows learners to generate context-sensitive criteria which can be interpreted in ways appropriate to the specific level of the learners.

Task: Write a review of a film adaptation of "A Family Supper". Remember to add relevant information about the director and the actors.

Film Review – A Family Supper

After five years, David Lynch, director of widely lauded films such as Mulholland Drive and Twin peaks has finally returned. With the adaptation of A Family Supper, a short story by Kazuo Ishiguro, Lynch has created another enigmatic and surreal, yet entirely compelling masterpiece. A Family Supper is the disturbing story of a Japanese family that is haunted by the ghosts of the past, problems of the present and the uncertainties of the future.

Two years after his mother's death, Jakeshi, a young Japanese man who had emigrated to California, returns to his mother country in order to visit his father and sister. It's late already when he arrives at his father's house. Suddenly Jakeshi believes he has seen a mysterious woman clad in a white kimono disappear behind the house. He follows her but she's gone. This is only the first instance of a bone-chilling evening full of despair, fear, pain and insanity that awaits Jakeshi.

As in most other movies by David Lynch, the story-line is entirely impenetrable and impossible to interpret. However, A Family Supper is atmospheric and transmits the characters' emotions in an effective yet unconventional way. The film's atmosphere was generally supported by Howard Shore's brilliant score and the extra-ordinary sound effects.

Most of the film was shot on location in a small town on Hokkaido, Japan. And also the cast is mostly Japanese. A Family Supper stars

---

1 Cf. ELTT rating scale for writing and benchmarked sample texts at http://www.uni-klu.ac.at/ltc/inhalt/430.htm.

> *Japan's most talented and renowned actor, Ken Watanabe, who gives an outstanding performance as the father. The main character Jakeshi is played by the up-and-coming Ishiguro Misaki, who depicts the character of Jakeshi in the most memorable way. 28-year-old Misaki gave his film debut in Kawasaki's epic drama The Lore of the Dragon. In Family Supper, he proves that he doesn't need special effects in order to perform well. Misaki is a brilliant actor who is able to depict mental as well as physical agony.*
>
> *Unfortunately, next to Watanabe's and Misaki's outstanding performances, Amy Kenobe's efforts to depict Kikuko remain largely unnoticed. Her acting qualities are pathetic and deserve no recognition. She is the only miscast in the movie.*
>
> *Despite Kenobe's disappointing performance, David Lynch's A Family Supper will certainly please his fans and supporters of surreal cinema. A Family Supper proves once again that Lynch is a genius, even if the products of this genius cannot be understood or interpreted.*

4. Possible variation

The idea underlying the schema can be adapted for specific purposes such as evaluating presentations, oral tasks and particular text types. In addition, students may wish to develop their own individual schema depending on their personal needs to monitor their own progress.

5. Annotated bibliography

Hyland K. and F. Hyland (eds.) (2006). *Feedback in Second Language Writing*. Cambridge: Cambridge University Press.
The editors have collected a variety of opinions on how effective feedback works, including views on peer review and on the use of electronic tools in feedback.

Kohonen, V. (1992). Experiential language learning: second language learning as cooperative learner education. In: D. Nunan (ed.) *Collaborative Language Learning and Teaching*. Cambridge: Cambridge University Press. 14 – 39.

This chapter offers a rich discussion of the theoretical background underlying experiential learning.

Nunan, D. (1997). Designing and adapting materials to encourage learner autonomy. In: P. Benson & P. Voller (eds.) *Autonomy & Independence in Language Learning.* London: Longman. 192 – 203.
This is an interesting theoretical chapter exploring ways of adapting materials for learner autonomy.

White, R. and V. Arndt (1991). *Process Writing.* Harlow: Longman.
A practical handbook involving a collaborative approach to the teaching of writing.

Webliography

Gabrielatos, C. (2002). EFL writing: Product and process. *ERIC,* ED 476839. http://www.gabrielatos.com/Writing.pdf [accessed 18.12.08]
An innovative article addressing writing in terms of product and process)

Martin, R. (2008). Using the Common European Framework for Self-Assessment in EFL Classes. http://www.ccu.edu.tw/fllcccu/2008EIA/English/C32.pdf [accessed: 18.12.08]
An interesting article describing research with EFL learners engaged in self-assessment using the CEF.

2.2. The *A*RT of Writing: *A*ppropriacy and *R*egister in *T*ext

Sarah Mercer and Jennifer Schumm

1. Rationale

One area that advanced learners often encounter difficulties with concerns appropriacy of register and style across different contexts. Therefore, students tend to need sensitising to the variations in lexical and syntactical choices depending on situation and audience in order to communicate effectively. The authors have found that learners often need to work on a wide range of text types and contexts in order to develop a better feeling for the various degrees of formality. However, care must be taken not to create a simplistic dichotomy between *either* formal *or* informal, but rather to emphasise the extent to which a text is more formal or informal. The following tasks are intended to make learners aware of degrees of formality and of subtle language variations in given contexts.

2. Procedure

(1) The students are given a handout with sentences and are asked to consider their level of formality on a continuum ranging from very informal to very formal. It is stressed that issues of register do not reflect a dichotomous division between either formal or informal, but are rather a question of the degree of formality. Students should think about a possible context in which the sentences might appear as well as the relationship between addresser and addressee. Students discuss their answers with a partner. For ease of comparison, the authors recommend that all the sentences have the same function, e.g., complaining, giving advice, apologising etc. (See example materials 1 for an example of possible sentences).

(2) After having discussed the sentences with a partner, students are asked to draw up a list of characteristics for more formal and informal language use. The whole class then discuss their ideas together

and responses are written up on the board. (See example materials 2 for possible answers).

(3) Moving from the sentence level to the text level, students, working in pairs, are given a series of cards containing short texts as well as information about the context of the text and addresser/addressee. At least one sentence per text does not use the appropriate register. Students are asked to identify the inappropriate sentence(s) and re-write accordingly. (See example materials 3 for text cards).

(4) After discussing possible solutions, students form new pairs and each pair is given one card. Each card contains a task that requires students to produce a whole text using an inappropriate register and style for the particular context and audience given. When completed, they exchange their finished texts and cards with another pair. They now have to re-write their neighbours' text in a more appropriate way according to the context given on the card. (See example materials 4 for possible cards).

3. Example materials

(1) Possible advice sentence continuums:

Giving Advice:
Decide where the following sentences lie on the scale of formality. Consider in which context you might hear/read them and also think about the possible relationship between addresser and addressee. Discuss your answers with a partner.
- I really think you ought to go for it!

Very informal_____Very formal

- We advise customers to watch their valuables carefully.

Very informal_____Very formal

- May we take this opportunity to advise you that this process is not officially recognised.

Very informal_____Very formal

- Why don't you just write her a letter?

Very informal_____Very formal

- After much careful consideration we would like to make the following recommendations.

Very informal_____Very formal

- I'm sure it's a great idea. I guess you should just try it out.

Very informal_____Very formal

- Have you ever considered spending a period of time abroad?

Very informal_____Very formal

- May I suggest that you re-word your proposal as I consider it highly inappropriate?

Very informal_____Very formal

<u>Observation:</u>
What do you notice about some of the characteristics of more informal and more formal language? Make a list here based on the examples here or on your own examples.

(2) Possible characteristics for more formal/ informal/language:

Typically more formal	*Typically more informal*
- Full form of verbs - Words of Latin/French origin - No contractions - Sentences that are obviously not from spoken language - Use of inversion for conditionals & emphasis - Formal connectors - Not ending sentence with preposition - Complex sentences	- Phrasal verbs - Colloquial vocabulary - Contractions - Sentences that sound close to spoken English - Question tags - Omission of subject - Informal connectors - Ending with preposition - Simple sentences

(Cf. Cory 1999: 14)

(3) Possible text cards:

Card A   Context: Email   Addresser/Addressee: Friends   Hi Sue – what's up? Haven't heard from u for ages so thought I'd drop you a line to see how you're doing. Just finished my summer job – what a drag!!!! Had to wait tables all summer long and the hours were pretty bad. However, we were treated extremely well by the patrons of the restaurant and were remunerated accordingly. Am planning to get back to uni soon so I can settle back in before semester starts. Might I suggest you contact me to arrange a meeting? It'd be great to meet up, so give me a call, will u?   Cu soon   Geoff
Card B   Context: Report for a company   Addresser/Addressee: Head of department – employee   This report is intended to outline the major factors involved in the current dispute with the union body. A study was conducted to identify the key grievances and demands. The study was based on a survey of nearly 200 employees based at the factory in Longbridge. I'm now going to tell you what I found out.   The first grievance concerns promotions. Numerous employees expressed their dissatisfaction at the lack of opportunities and support offered by the company at present. They complained that you don't take them seriously or give them a hand with getting on in their jobs. To this end, the request was made that additional support staff and professional development are offered at all levels.

Card C
Context: Job application cover letter
Addresser/Addressee: Prospective employer – candidate applying for job

Dear Sir or Madam,
I am writing with regard to the post of programmer advertised in the Guardian on the 13th November.
I am currently working for the FTW company as a junior programmer based in Stuttgart. My contract finishes at the end of this year and I would be interested in relocating to London.
My work experience has familiarised me with many of the challenges involved in computer programming today. My English is great thanks to plenty of holidays spent in GB. I'd guess these two things would make me the right guy for the job.
I would be pleased to discuss my curriculum vitae with you in more detail at an interview.
I look forward to hearing from you.
Yours faithfully,
John Bates

Card D
Context: Entry on a student networking site
Addresser/Addressee: Student – student

Well, didn't get a wink last night cuz I just finished exams!!! Yeah!!! Glad to have that all over!!! It's been a helluva few weeks!!!
Wanted to let you guys know about a big bash tomorrow at the dorms on Main. It's BYOB and the Twisters are gonna party with us!!! Wicked!!! Furthermore, it is possible to be accompanied by a guest of your choice. The more, the merrier!!!
Hope to c u guys. We would be delighted to make your acquaintance and have the pleasure of spending the evening together.
Stormin' Norman

Key:
Card A:
"However, we were treated extremely well by the patrons of the restaurant and were remunerated accordingly."
Suggested possible re-write:
Still, the owners treated us pretty well and the pay was cool.
"Might I suggest you contact me to arrange a meeting?"
Suggested possible re-write:
Let's get in touch and plan to meet up.

Card B:
"I'm now going to tell you what I found out."
Suggested possible re-write:
I shall now outline the findings of the survey.
"They complained that you don't take them seriously or give them a hand with getting on in their jobs."
Suggested possible re-write:
Specifically, employees complained that management did not appear to value or support staff in their careers.

Card C:
"My English is great thanks to plenty of holidays spent in GB. I'd guess these two things would make me the right guy for the job."
Suggested possible re-write:
As a result of several periods of time spent in Britain, I have developed excellent English language skills. I believe that these two qualities would make me ideally suited to the position offered.

Card D:
"Furthermore, it is possible to be accompanied by a guest of your choice."
Suggested possible re-write:
Bring along a friend!
"We would be delighted to make your acquaintance and have the pleasure of spending the evening together."
Suggested possible re-write:
Can't wait to get to meet up and hang out 2gether!

(4) Possible cards:

CARD A Context: *Email* Addresser/Addressee: *Friends* Purpose: *To invite them to a party*	CARD B Context: *Abstract of a seminar paper* Addresser/Addressee: *Professor – student* Purpose: *To outline the content of seminar paper*
CARD C Context: *Love letter* Addresser/Addressee: *Couple in long-distance relationship* Purpose: *To share feelings and reassure*	CARD D Context: *Letter of complaint* Addresser/Addressee: *Store owner – customer* Purpose: *To complain about a faulty TV*

4. Possible variation

The activities can be adapted to focus on specific functions and text types. A wider range of sentences and text types are generally needed to help students to fully appreciate and develop a deeper understanding of appropriacy and register in text.

5. Annotated bibliography

Cory, H. (1999). *Advanced Writing with English in Use.* Oxford: Oxford University Press.
   A coursebook for advanced learners that addresses issues of genre and key areas of writing, especially register.
O'Dell, F. (1996). *CAE Writing Skills.* Cambridge: Cambridge University Press.
   A practical book covering a range of writing skills with an emphasis on register and appropriacy.
Stephens, M. (1992). *Practise Advanced Writing.* Harlow: Longman.
   A practical book for advanced learners focusing on text type and addressing register.

2.3. Developing an Awareness of the Communicative Nature of Writing

Sarah Mercer and Jennifer Schumm

1. Rationale

Whilst being aware of the communicative purpose involved in speaking, many students often overlook this element in written texts. The following set of activities has been designed to raise student awareness of the communicative aspect of writing and to sensitise them to the similarities and differences involved in written and spoken communication. At the core of the series of activities is the concept of communicating your message effectively – whether it be via speech or the written word.

2. Procedure

(1) In small groups, learners discuss statements about communication in order to reflect on elements involved in communicating successfully both in writing and speaking. (See example materials 1 for possible discussion questions).
(2) After groups report back on their discussions, students get into pairs for a role play. They are given cards with their roles and context. All the students sit face-to-face and take part in a Skype video call with their partner. Mid-way through their call, the teacher announces that, due to a technical fault, the line has broken down and they must continue their conversation via messenger. For this second stage, students turn back-to-back and in silence pass messages written on paper back and forth to each other. (See example materials 2 for role play cards).
(3) As a follow-up activity to the role play, the whole class is asked to consider in what ways the dynamics changed following the switch from spoken to written communication. Together the group draws up a list on the board of similarities and differences between the two

forms of communication. Emphasis should be placed on the fact that both involve communicating a message in some way.

(4) In pairs, learners are then given a selection of 4 texts which they should analyse in respect to their communicative purpose. (See example materials 3 for discussion questions and texts). Two of the texts fail to communicate effectively. Students should then suggest how they could be re-worked in order to be more communicatively effective.

(5) In the final stage, each student receives an instruction card with an outline for a written task. After producing a written piece that should reflect the characteristics outlined on the card, the learners exchange their texts with a partner. On reading their partner's written piece, each student should try to identify the characteristics which their partner was given on their instruction card. The points on the cards are as follows:

- Text type
- Communicative purpose
- Messenger
- Receiver
- Relationship

The characteristics identified by their partner will indicate to what extent the written piece was successful in achieving its communicative purpose. (See example materials 4 for role play cards).

3. Example materials

(1) Example of possible communication statements:

> Consider the following statements. To what extent do you agree or disagree with the statements (1 = disagree strongly, 10 = agree strongly)? Be prepared to discuss reasons for your opinion.
> a) *Communicating is sending and receiving the right messages.*
> b) *Using body language to get your message across is a sign of being a poor communicator.*

> c) A good communicator is human and shows empathy.
> d) If you express yourself clearly, there is no need to check you have been understood properly.
> e) Successful communication depends more on the sender than the receiver of the message.
> f) Interaction is not necessary for communication.

(2) Example of possible role play cards:

ROLE A	ROLE B
You are a student spending a year abroad in London. You are skyping with a friend of yours from your home university who is currently studying in Dublin. At first, you talk about your experiences and highs and lows of the stay so far. You then decide to make plans to meet up in Edinburgh for the New Year Hogmanay festival. Arrange and finalise details of your trip before you hang up.	You are a student spending a year abroad in Dublin. You are skyping with a friend of yours from your home university who is currently studying in London. At first, you talk about your experiences and highs and lows of the stay so far. You then decide to make plans to meet up in Edinburgh for the New Year Hogmanay festival. Arrange and finalise details of your trip before you hang up.

(3) Examples of discussion questions & texts:

- What is the text type?
- What is the communicative purpose of each text?
- To what extent has it achieved its purpose from the reader's perspective? Why?
- Who are the messenger & receiver involved in this act of communication? What is their relationship?

TEXT A	TEXT B
The two brothers, Emerson & Evan Covington, who have recently opened 'Creole Kid' offer a wide selection of excellent Cajun cuisine. They have taken some classics and added their own personal touch. Their thick and spicy gumbo served with a garden fresh salad is simply irresistible. And don't miss their luscious, mouth-watering pecan pie which is a speciality of the house. A family-friendly place with a warm, inviting atmosphere. Make sure you book your table in advance.	Dear Emerson & Evan, I'm thoroughly disgusted at the service and gross food you served at your place last night. You should be ashamed of yourselves and I think I should get my money back. If I don't, you can expect to hear from my lawyer. Yours, John Smith

PS. You serve a fantastic pecan pie! |
| **TEXT C** CAJUN SCRAMBLED EGGS Serve with chapatti bread. Do not let the egg mixture dry out in the pan. Stir in the milk and add the remaining ingredients. Beat the eggs well before putting in the pan. Cook over low heat for no longer than two minutes. Eggs Milk 2 green chillies 1 teaspoon ginger 1 teaspoon turmeric Tomato S & P | **TEXT D** *CREOLE KID* The hottest Cajun restaurant in Boston. Southern cooking at its best – prepared with a unique, special flair. The gumbo is divine and the desserts are to die for – don't miss the memorable pecan pie. Reasonably priced meals – specials for families. Come visit us soon for an unforgettable 'down-south' dining experience. For reservations call: 419 – 6233 |

Key:

Text B and C fail in their communicative purpose.
B in terms of register, style, tone and content.
C in terms of structure, layout, organisation and content.

(4) Examples of written task instructions:

Writing Task A Text type: Tourist brochure Communicative purpose: To attract visitors to your home town Messenger: Town tourist office Receiver: English-speaking tourists Relationship: Distant/unknown	Writing Task B Text type: Letter of application for summer job Communicative purpose: To create a good impression and gain an interview for the job Messenger: You Receiver: Head of Personnel at the company Relationship: Distant/unknown
Writing Task C Text type: Instructions Communicative purpose: To describe how students register for courses at this university Messenger: Student counselling service Receiver: First year undergraduate students Relationship: Neutral	Writing Task D Text type: Film review Communicative purpose: To express your opinion about the film Messenger: Student newspaper reviewer Receiver: Student readers of newspaper Relationship: Neutral

4. Possible variation

All the text types can be adapted with a focus on specific text types and genre. The writing/speaking dichotomy can also be explored in more depth with further examples.

5. Annotated bibliography

Byrne, D. (1988). *Teaching Writing Skills*. Harlow: Longman.
   A practical book that offers a communicative approach to the teaching of writing.

Cory, H. (1999). *Advanced Writing with English in Use.* Oxford: Oxford University Press.
A coursebook that addresses issues of genre and key areas of writing.

Nuttall, C. (1996). *Teaching Reading Skills in a Foreign Language.* Oxford: Heinemann.
A theoretical and practical book that emphasises the communicative function of text.

3. Words into Text

Introduction to Section 3

Adult language learners who have already achieved a certain level of proficiency in the target language tend to groan when they hear the word grammar. Often they cannot see the link between communicatively effective language production and grammar. One reason for this missing link seems to be that conventional grammar practice formats rarely take the learners beyond sentence level; another is that grammar is frequently taught with a focus on isolated functions and notions. This is why learners tend to get things right when exercises focus explicitly on certain structures but fail to do so when producing texts. Thus, teachers are faced with fossilization and other forms of ingrained erroneous language habits, and their difficult task is to motivate learners to question the hypotheses that they have built up about the systems of the target language.

This section of the book offers three practice approaches. The first two aim at making learners aware of how, in text creation, lexico-grammatical features combine to fulfil a communicative purpose, thus re-enforcing acceptable concepts and challenging erroneous hypotheses. The third format focuses on a strategy that aims at training learners' ability to analyse and self-assess their own text production by taking text-constituent factors into account.

The first practice approach introduced in chapter 3.1 is WIT (*Words into Texts*). It involves learners in text creation and at the same time focuses on specific grammatical aspects. WIT is a highly flexible practice approach that can be adapted to serve a variety of learner needs. It can assist learners in discovering the information structure of an English text, for example, by leaving the decision to the learner of which tense to use or whether to use active or passive voice.

The second approach, the so-called grammar story strategy, is presented in chapter 3.2 (*Grammar Stories: Teaching of Notional Grammar through Interactive Story-Telling*).This approach is an interactive one, the purpose of which is to help learners discover superstructures, i.e. lexico-grammatical patterns that are typical of certain text types. Moreover, grammar stories encourage learners to experiment with these super-

tures. The chapter also shows how the texts that learners produce can be shared and evaluated collaboratively, by using electronic tools and by setting up task-specific learner corpora.

Finally, chapter 3.3 (*AIDA: from Text Analysis to Context-Sensitive Text Production*) explains the "A-I-D-A" strategy, which is based on a popular marketing technique. It guides learners towards self-assessment not only of the finished product but also of their individual learning needs and learning options. The "A-I-D-A" strategy is particularly useful for learners who need to produce purpose-oriented texts that have some persuasive function.

3.1. WIT (Words Into Text)

Margit Reitbauer and Renate Vaupetitsch

1. Rationale

WIT assists learners in their progression from an intermediate to an advanced level of language use because it allows learners to take an active part in text creation and helps them to realise how various lexico-grammatical features combine in meaningful discourse[1]. As WIT is designed to make learners aware of lexico-grammatical choices, they are thus better equipped to take informed decisions when constructing texts themselves. In addition this new approach stimulates new thinking about texts from a holistic perspective[2].

The advantage of WIT is that it can be adapted easily to focus on a great variety of teaching objectives. The focus can be specifically on tense, voice, aspect, modality, collocation, etc. or on a combination of various grammar features. For example, a story can be used to focus on past simple/past progressive and effective use of vivid verbs, or a letter of application for an au pair job can be analysed to highlight complex tense use and examples of verb complementation. WIT also assists learners in discovering the information structure of an English text, for example, by leaving the decision of whether to use active or passive voice to the learners.

---

1 It could be argued that cloze tasks perform a similar function. In the *New First Certificate Coursebook GOLD* (2004), for example, quite a few multiple choice and open clozes are offered. The cloze tasks focus on text as well but they do not involve the learner in text creation to the extent that WIT does and they do not allow a clear focus on particular grammar features. More often than not the cloze tasks highlight vocabulary and cohesion rather than grammar, and they are, above all, a tool to test, in particular, a tool to test comprehension.
2 This approach is used occasionally, in Hewings (2005), for example, where the instructions are expand and use, but only in a few single sentences rather than across a whole text.

2. Procedure

(1) Use the CEFR descriptors to specify the learner needs of your target groups.
(2) Choose a text type that naturally makes use of the lexico-grammatical features that need to be focused upon. (see example materials 1 and 2).
(3) Choose either authentic texts or texts constructed by the teacher or texts from text books (see example materials 2 and 4). It is also possible to use learner texts produced in previous courses or produced by learners in the same course (see example materials 3). Learners enjoy being allowed to contribute to text creation by, for example, providing their own ending (see example materials 4).
(4) Analyse examples of the relevant text type together with the learners to help them understand the lexico-grammatical features of this text type (see chapter 3.3 on "A-I-D-A").
(5) Break up the text into words or chunks: what is taken out and what is left depends on the task focus. If the task focus is tense use, only the base forms of verbs are left. To increase learners' awareness of cohesion, it is useful to leave out function words, determiners, etc.
(6) Ask learners to put **WORDS INTO TEXT** by following the basic instructions for learners. These instructions may have to be extended or modified depending on the task and the task focus (see example materials 5).

3. Example materials

(1) Focus: tense use and verb complementation

This is an application letter for an au pair job in England. The writer has been asked to explain why s/he wants to do the job.

Try to reconstruct the following text from the words given; you will have to change verb forms and add function words to make this a meaningful and idiomatic text.

Dear Mrs. Browning,

I / write / because / I / like / to apply / au pair job / that / you / advertise / last week's paper. I / finish / school / last year / and / I / study / English / university. But / before / I / take up / my studies / I / like / spend / year abroad. Taking a year out / help / me / get / clearer view of myself / and / I / think / it's time / I / see / a bit of the world.

I / apply / au pair job / your family / two reasons. First / I / always / enjoy / look / children /. I / be / not / professionally trained nanny / but / I / do / quite a lot / babysitting / last two years. I / know / it / be / hard work, / and / if / I / look / holiday / I / not / apply / au pair job.

The other reason / be / that / I / want / go / English-speaking country / ever since / I / start / learn /English. It/ be / English assistant teacher / at school / who / encourage / me / take up English studies. And she / suggest / work / as an au pair. She / argue / that as an au pair / I / live / a family / and / thus / I / be / able / experience /England / more profoundly / than / if / I / go / there / as a tourist.

In your letter / you / say / you / need / somebody / August to August, / which / suit / me / nicely / because / I / like / do / some travelling / September / once / job / be / over.

I / be / grateful if / you / can /send / me / more information regarding working hours and pay.

Yours sincerely, …

(2) Focus: information structure [use of passive/ active voice]

Try to reconstruct the following text from the words give. You will have to change verb forms and add function words to make this a meaningful and idiomatic text.

Volcano Eruption

A volcano has erupted on a Pacific island. It had lain dormant for over 200 years until yesterday. Here is the report from last night's 9 o'clock news.

Here I am standing at the top of a pile of rubble. Yesterday it was a school. Over 50 people / dig out / so far, / only a few / be / still / alive / when / they / find.

Volcano / erupt / just as / everyone / sleepy little town / have / breakfast. Some / kill / blast and the heat. Some / kill / when / houses / collapse / – / they / bury/ alive / rubble. Children / kill /as / they / drive / their schools / their parents. Most of the people /who / die / say / be born / here. It may be weeks / before / it / know / how many people / kill. The effects of the eruption / report / be felt / people living many miles from the scene.

A state of emergency / declare / and / the surviving population / tell / not to move back into their houses. Tents / put up / currently / provide / shelter for the homeless/ as / rain and a drop in temperature / forecast / next few days.

As we / look out / this scene of chaos / in the midst / beautiful hills and mountains / it is difficult to believe / what / happen. Lives /that / used / happy / ruin; families / split up; a whole community / destroy. It / ever / rebuild?

This is Michael Buck for the 9 o'clock news at the scene of the disaster.

Text based on exercise (text-based questions) from Jimmie Hill / Rosalyn Hurst, *Grammar and Practice.* (1989). Hove: LTP, p.97.

(3) Hypo Stories: Focus on hypothetical tense use

The following texts are based on stories that students created in group work:

Try to reconstruct the following text from the words given; you will have to change verb forms and add function words to make this a meaningful and idiomatic text.

Sample HYPO STORY:

> If only I hadn't told him that I was American.
>   I wish he would stop phoning me and begging me to see his friend from Los Angeles.
>   I'd rather he didn't send me those love letters in English.
>   It's time he realized that I'm from Deutschlandsberg.

If only I / know /where I am.
   I wish I / not / drink / quite as much last night.
     I'd rather / I / remember / how / I get / this room.
      It's time somebody / tell / me / what / happen / last night.

If only I / not / have / chat / chat-room /him.
   I wish I / not / give / him / my e-mail address.
     I'd rather he / not / send / me / such / lurid /pictures.
      It's time he / realise / I am a man.

I wish I / attend / course / last week.
   If only I / know / what we / have / prepare / for today.
     It's time somebody / tell / me / what is going on.
      I'd rather they / not / look / me / in such a funny way.

(4) Focus on past simple / progressive

Task a)
Reconstruct "A Sad Story" from the words given; use only past simple or past progressive tenses. You will also have to provide articles and prepositions to make this a meaningful text.

A Sad Story

In September 1988 / Mr and Mrs Smith / live / top floor flat / high-rise building. One day / Mrs Smith / be / home. It / be / beautiful day, / and / sun / shine / and / town below/ people / enjoy / good weather. While Mrs Smith / look / window/ she / see / her husband / walk / building. Just when / he / get/ lift/ she / open / door,/ very surprised to see him home so early from the office. He/ tell / his wife / that / he / leave / her.

Of course, Mrs Smith / be / shocked and upset. While he / put / his clothes / suitcase/ Mrs Smith / cry. She /still / cry / when he / walk / door.

Mrs Smith / listen / while / lift / go / down. When / it / stop / ground floor/ she / walk / window,/ open / it / ...

Task b)

What could be a possible ending to the story? Finish the story by writing a few sentences.

Text based on exercise (text-based questions) from:
Hill, J. and R. Hurst (1989). *Grammar and Practice*. Hove: LTP. 97.

(5) Instructions for learners:

➢ Skim-read the WIT script.
➢ Analyse the underlying organisational pattern of the text.
➢ Put **WORDS INTO TEXT** by constructing a meaningful text from the words given and by keeping the text type and its lexico-grammatical needs in mind.
➢ Compare with model text.
➢ Consider possible meaningful variations.

Key to example materials

1

Dear Mrs Browning,

I am writing because I would like to apply for the au pair job you advertised in last week's paper. I finished school last year and I am going to study English at the university. But before I take up my studies I would like to spend a year abroad. Taking a year out will help me (to) get a clearer view of myself and I think it is time I saw a bit of the world.

I am applying for the au pair job with your family for two reasons. First I have always enjoyed looking after children. I am not a professionally trained nanny, but I have done quite a lot of babysitting in the last two years. I know it is hard work, and if I were looking for a holiday, I would not apply for an au pair job.

The other reason is that I have wanted to go to an English-speaking country ever since I started learning English. It was an English assistant teacher at school who encouraged me to take up English studies. And she suggested working (suggested that I should work) as an au pair. She argued that as an au pair I would be living with a family and thus I would be able to experience England more profoundly than if I went there as a tourist.

In your letter you say that you need somebody from August to August, which suits me nicely because I would like to do some travelling in September, once the job is over.

I would be grateful if you could send me more information regarding working hours and pay.

Yours sincerely,

2

A volcano has erupted on a Pacific island. It had lain dormant for over 200 years until yesterday. Here is the report from last night's 9 o'clock news:

Here I am standing at the top of a pile of rubble. Yesterday it was a school. Over 50 people have been dug out so far, only a few were still alive when they were found.

The volcano erupted just as everyone in the sleepy little town was having breakfast. Some were killed by the blast and the heat. Some were killed when their houses collapsed – they were buried alive in the rubble. Children were killed as they were being driven to their schools by their parents. Most of the people who died are said to have been born here. It may be weeks before it is known how many people were killed. The effects of the eruption were felt by people living many miles from the scene.

A state of emergency has been declared and the surviving population has been told not to move back as rain and a drop in temperature are forecast for (in) the next few days.

As we look (are looking) out at this scene of chaos in the midst of beautiful hills and mountains, it is difficult to believe what has happened. Lives that used to be happy are (have been) ruined; families are (have been) split up; a whole community has been destroyed. Will it ever be rebuilt?

This is Michael Buck for the 9 o'clock news at the scene of the disaster.

3

If only I knew where I am.
    I wish I hadn't drunk quite as much last night.
    I'd rather I could remember how I got into this room.
        It's time somebody told me what happened last night.

If only I hadn't had a chat in the chat-room with him.
    I wish I hadn't given him my e-mail address.
        I'd rather he didn't send me such lurid pictures.
            It's time he realised that I am a man.

I wish I'd attended the course last week.
    If only I knew what we had to prepare for today.
        It's time somebody told me what is going on.
            I'd rather they didn't all look at me in such a funny way.

4

A sad story

In September 1988 Mr. and Mrs. Smith were living in the top floor flat of a high-rise building. One day Mrs. Smith was at home. It was a beautiful day, the sun was shining and in the town below (the) people were enjoying the good weather. While Mrs Smith was looking out of the window, she saw her husband walking into the building. Just when he got out of the lift, she opened the door, very surprised to see him home so early from the office. He told his wife that he was leaving her.

Of course, Mrs. Smith was shocked and upset. While he was putting his clothes into a suitcase, Mrs. Smith was crying. She was still crying when he walked out of the door.

Mrs. Smith was listening while the lift was going down. When it stopped at (on) the ground floor, she walked to the window, opened it

> Ending of the original story:
> ... and jumped. At that exact moment, Mr. Smith walked out of the building. He was not thinking of his wife; he was thinking of his new life, when suddenly Mrs. Smith landed on top of him. He was killed instantly but Mrs Smith was completely unhurt. People said she was smiling when she recovered from the shock, but I'm not sure if that is true.

4. Possible variations

As already pointed out in the introduction and illustrated by examples, WIT can be used to focus on one single grammatical notion or, even more effectively, on a variety of notions and how they combine in a text.

5. Annotated bibliography

Han, Z. H. (2004). *Fossilization in Adult Second Language Acquisition.* Clevedon: Multilingual Matters.
  This book investigates in detail the phenomenon of fossilization, which is of particular importance in adult language learning.
Hall, N and J.Shepheard (2008). *The Anti-Grammar Grammar Book.* Brighton: ELB Publishing.
  This new edition of a popular book focuses on pair and group work and encourages inductive learning through problem-solving activities.
Hewings, M. (2005). *Advanced Grammar in Use.* Cambridge: Cambridge University Press. (See footnote 2)
Hill, J. and R., Hurst (1989). *Grammar and Practice.* Hove: LTP.
  Although quite traditionally structuralist in its approach, the self-study book for intermediate learners of English offers a large variety

of exercises which definitely have some fun factor as well (jokes, drawings, grids, etc.).

Hillier, E. (1983). *Grammar and Vocabulary*. London: Collins ELT.
The book caters for the needs of students who want to study scientific subjects through the medium of English. The book works with authentic text passages from printed sources, and through completion, substitution and dictionary exercises aims at increasing vocabulary but also making learners aware of the functions of grammatical elements. The book is a result of the writer's experience in preparing students for the Cambridge and Joint Matriculation Board Examinations in the 1970s.

Newbrook J., J.Wilson and R. Acklam (2004). *New First Certificate Coursebook GOLD*. Harlow: Pearson Longman. (See footnote 1)

Webliography

Council of Europe: Common European Framework of Reference for Languages: Learning, Teaching, Assessment. http://www.coe.int/T/DG4/Linguistic/CADRE_EN.asp [accessed 21.12.2008]
The website allows access to the complete text of the CEFR.

3.2. Grammar Stories: Teaching Notional Grammar through Interactive Story-Telling

Margit Reitbauer und Renate Vaupetitsch

1. Rationale

The telling of stories seems to be a basic human need, so it is not surprising that stories play an important role in EFL methodology. In traditional grammar teaching the focus has been mainly on reception rather than production. 'Grammar story-telling', in contrast, approaches notional grammar with real story magic and focuses on interactive production within the setting of an electronic platform.

Grammar stories are based on a real world communication task and help learners to find solutions by looking at the nature of grammar in use in story clusters rather than individual elements of structure. Grammar stories can be used to focus on a variety of grammatical notions. It has been found that this strategy is most effective when the objective is to show how two or more grammatical notions combine in a text (e.g. the event notion and the accompanying circumstances notions in past narratives, various modality notions, etc.). In addition, contextualisation in the form of stories can have positive mnemonic effects.

Another reason for using grammar stories is that learners who create their own stories after analysing the narrative superstructure of texts normally become aware of how various grammatical notions are combined in story-telling and thus can make informed decisions in their own writing. Furthermore, learners can apply the findings of interactive peer discourse research and feedback to the design of their own stories; thus, discovery learning and deductive reasoning can be enhanced.

There are obviously no keys or solutions to these tasks since the evaluation of the stories takes place interactively through a peer audience that is aware of the underlying superstructures of the texts. The authors have found that these peer reviews can be done most effectively by using learning platforms like WebCT.

2. Procedure

(1) Choose a model text that illustrates the grammar notions that you want to focus on (e.g. past ability). Texts previously produced by learners and then chosen by their peers have proved to be particularly useful models (see example materials on instructions for learners and three sample texts).
(2) Devise a superstructure of the text together with the learners (see example materials 2). For comparison, a superstructure of a learner biography has also been included (see example materials 3).
(3) Ask learners to write their own stories (either experience-based or fictional), keeping the superstructure and the lexico-grammatical needs of their text in mind.
(4) Tell learners to use the superstructure of the text during peer conferencing. Feedback can be even more effective if a feedback grid is negotiated previously with the learners (see chapter 3.3).
(5) Use electronic tools, if possible, for interactive story-telling (e.g. learning platforms like WebCT). The text analysis can also be facilitated by employing learner corpora (see example materials 4).

3. Example materials

(1) These instructions can be used for analysis of the texts below.

- Skim-read the model text.
- Analyse the text and establish its superstructure (see example materials 2).
- Write your own story, based on the superstructure that you have established.
- Post your story on the learning platform.
- Ask your peers to read your story and give you constructive feedback.

The following sample stories deal with the notions of potential past ability and actual application of past ability.

Text 1: *Buffalos*
There was nothing to see but dust, raised by heavy hoofs, and nothing to hear but the trampling of the buffalo herd. They were chasing something that had really made them angry. But what was it? Buffalos normally only get angry if someone tries to steal their food, but there were enough pastures for all of them.

Suddenly the noise stopped. The buffalos had come to a halt. Slowly the dust settled again. In front of the herd one could already make out the silhouette of a person, a very small one though. It was a child, a little native American boy. His sudden stop had obviously startled the buffalos so much that they also pulled up. "Please," he cried, "Don't chase me! I only wanted to play with your cute buffalo babies." But the animals didn't understand. No one was allowed to touch their offspring. They were just about to start the chase again when all of a sudden the little boy roared like a real buffalo. He could imitate this sound perfectly. Fortunately his father had taught him how to do it in case of an unpleasant encounter with those straggly animals. And with his roar he managed to stop the herd from attacking him.

From then on the little boy was accepted as part of the buffalo herd. He could come and play with the buffalo babies as often as he wanted.

Text 2: *Jackie and the Monster Kitten*
None of my eight legs was missing. I could feel my body and I was still able to move. Did that mean that I did not have to leave this world at the tender age of three weeks? I was alive! Thank God! Never before had I experienced such terrible fear, mortal fear, fear of being killed by a monster kitten.

Like every morning I crawled from the corner of the cellar where my family lives to my friend's place at the opposite one. We have known each other for all our lives – three weeks that is – and spend most of our days together. It was him who had shown me the trick due to which I survived the kitten's attack. Thus, when I was only two days old I could already stand as motionless and stiff as a stone so that my mother once thought I was dead. This morning, however, this trick saved my life. Having almost arrived at my destination I heard a men-

acing purr behind me. I knew what it was but nonetheless turned around to see how close the danger was and to consider whether there was any sense in fleeing. And there it was, right behind me: a gigantic grey-striped kitten with huge paws and sparkling sharp teeth. I did not even attempt to escape – it would have been senseless because the kitten could run a thousand times faster than I could. My body was shaking. This apparently stimulated the kitten for then it hit me with its enormous paw. I flew through the air but fortunately landed on my feet. Then my friend's trick came to my mind: I took heart and stood stiff as a poker. I did not even allow myself to breathe. Thus, I managed to fake my death. The kitten came closer, touched me with its paw, rolled me on my back and – since I was not moving – lost interest in playing with me and trotted off.

Now my family and friends call me 'Stiff Jackie' and all the spiders in our cellar want me to teach their children my survival tactics. Thinking it over now, though, I am sure I would have been able to fight the kitten. It was not that big.

Text 3: *An Autumn Adventure*
It was a bright, windy morning in early autumn, when some trees were beginning to adorn themselves with different shades of warm colours while others were still lingering in the green-leaved state of summer time; the sun had already done half of its daily stint and blinkered curiously through the slender trees which groaned under the wild wind. On a day like this the little girl loved to go outside and spend hours flying her deltoid-shaped kite, watching its long tail curving restlessly through the air. She could fly her kite quite well without any help from her father, who wasn't able to get out this day to join her because he was suffering from a migraine attack. The kite danced joyously in the sky, borne upon the wind, and the girl's mind was exalted from happiness to an adventurous excitement which she had not known before. The kite had to fly higher and faster, had to perform more risky pirouettes! And then suddenly its flight came to an end. It had been pinned onto a pointy twig of a tree and twitched like a wild animal caught in a trap while its long tail hung motionless from the trunk of the tree as if all the joy had yielded to sadness. The girl stood still for a moment until she had calmed down and then ran to the tree

to set her friend free. She could climb up all the trees in her garden but this one was on the other side of the fence and its trunk was very thick and too smooth for climbing. But she had to try, she had to! Nobody was there to help her, her father being inside her house and the neighbours on a weekend vacation. The kite winced as if in pain. This made the girl try to climb on the wire netting fence, which seemed to retreat under her weight as if to hypocritically interfere with the rescue attempt. But she managed to get hold of a bough of the tree next to the one which had captivated her kite and was able to pull herself up until she was on eye level with her friend.

At first she tried to reach the kite with her fingers, but the branch she was clinging to got thinner towards the end and she did not dare to move any further. She only noticed then that the pointy twig had pierced exactly the middle of the kite right where its heart would have been, which made her both sad and furious. After some time she eventually managed to break off a long thin bough and with its help she was able to reach her kite and break the pointy twig onto which her kite had been pinned. The kite sailed to the ground and waited for the girl to climb down the helpful tree. The girl took the kite inside her house and carefully put a huge, coloured tape on its wound. Her father, who had come out of his room to take a tablet, smiled and wondered why all little girls liked to nurse their things instead of exploring the adventures of their daily lives.

(2) Past ability: superstructure

This is the superstructure of a story that tells how somebody made use of the abilities [*managed to / was(were) able) to*] that s/he had acquired and possessed [*could*] to cope with a difficult situation.

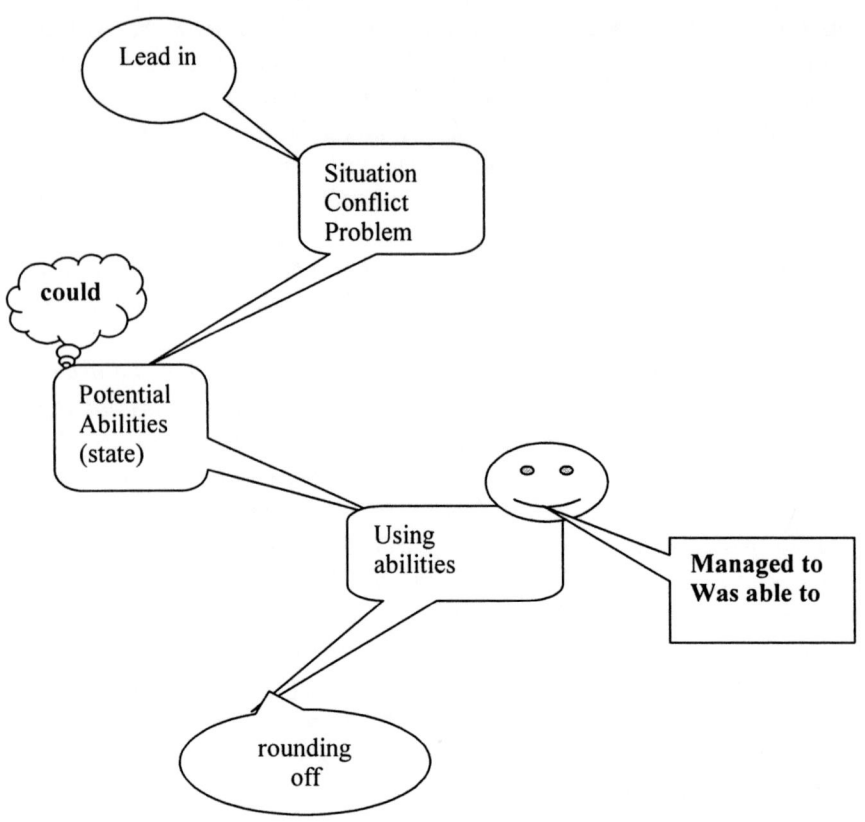

(3) Learner biography: superstructure. The text is entitled: Why English?

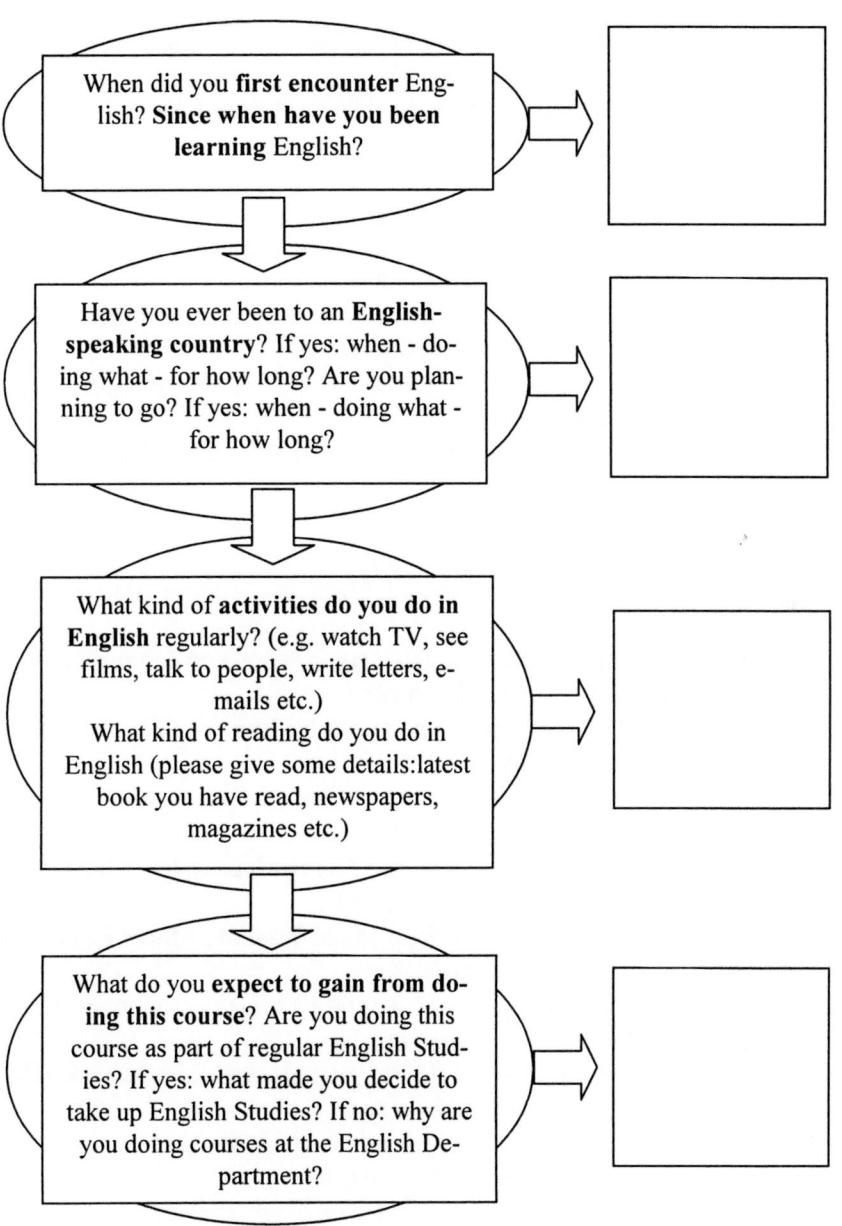

(4) Learner corpora

1. studies and what I expect from doing this course. I **have been** learning English since 9 years.
2. learning English since nine years. The first time I **have been** confronted with English skills in primary school
3. make very many experiences with the language. I **have been** to Malta two times. First time with my English
4. brought us English songs, comics or short poems. I **have been** learning English for eight years and I always
5. as a student exchange. I have many friends who **have been** to England for at least six months and they all told
6. The first time I noticed that English exists must **have been** when I started reading. I read out loud
7. dies for half a year! I don't want to go to England. I **have been** to England once, when I was in the 8th grade.
8. had to do some extra work. If you ask me if I ever **have been** to an English speaking country , I can only
9. to learn English in primary school. Until now I **have been** learning English for ten years.
10. ve been learning English for ten years. Moreover I **have been** to Great Britain. My class and I stayed in
11. sang songs and sometimes watched videos.I **have been** learning English for eleven years now and I
12. times. In the third class of secondary school I **have been** in Lancing (that's near Brighton) for one week.
13. as in Wellington, a little village near Greenwhich. I **have been** there for three weeks and I really saw a lot of
14. in Wales exactly in a small village called Henllan. I **have been** there for three weeks with my boyfriend.
15. one exactly in the first years of learning English. I **have been** learning English for about 10 years now, but
16. ut from my point of view he did not give his best. I **have been** fascinated by English very much, because I
17. for the first time on my own. All together I **have been** to the southcoast of the green isle 5 times for 3 weeks
18. WHY ENGLISH? I **have been** learning English since the first year of secondary school.

19 at the age of eight in the elementary school. I **have been** learning English for 11 years.
20 because it is such a long time ago... I must **have been** four or five years old. I just remember when our

1   I enjoy it to be there it can take a year or longer. **Since** then I try to do activities in English. I like to listen to
3   from doing this course. I have been learning English **since** nine years. The first time I have been confronted
4   on to take up this course was – in a way – not mine, **since** EG 1 is obligatory, but I am looking forward to
5   but rather because dubbed movies bother me a bit **since** I saw how different some jokes and sayings are in the
6   I am sure that I still need to work on my grammar **since** most of my spoken English is more or less slang.
7   for me to understand and learn languages but **since** my English lessons in primary school I have known that
8   songs and doing a little bit of conversation, and **since** we all enjoyed singing, we enjoyed English. At High
9   in a small village, in upper Styria, called Krieglach. **Since** this summer I reside here in Graz, in a small, cosy
10 University. It may sound kind of funny, but **since** I was a little girl, I have always had a strong "desire"
11 on I almost couldn't wait for the summer to come **since** this was the time I could go abroad to join a language
12 WHY ENGLISH? I have been learning English **since** the first year of secondary school. The only time I was
13 English? Well, I've been learning English regularly **since** I started attending High School. In this connection
14 learning English. Now, I've been learning English **since** ten years. Two years ago I went to Malta with my
15 and above all the hospitality of the English people. **Since** I have been a little girl I have always been dreaming
16 "strange" words. I have been learning English **since** the age of eight years. The English we learned at the
17 they didn't expect me to plan such a big trip, **since** I have always been a very family-oriented and homesick

18 all the British students I got to know in Worthing. **Since** my stay in the United Kingdom I really enjoy
19 foreign lanes, such as French, Latin and Spanish. **Since** then I didn't stop attending English lessons for ten
20 shopping center or collecting jokes on the street. **Since** then I try to keep a certain standard of English by
21 lazy. I have to confess that one year went by **since** I read the main works of Oscar Wilde as a preparation
22 in primary school, and I've been learning English **since**, altogether 11 years. I had one year in the last class
23 my grammar skills. I really have forgotten a lot **since** I learnt that thinks in school, but I'am sure that I'am up

4. Possible variations

For learners who need more guidance, a clear focus on particular grammatical structures can have a positive mnemonic effect. Stories based on performative verbs can be used to help learners remember verb complementation.

Travel Advice

Write an article for a student magazine giving advice to students who want to go backpacking abroad.

Please organise your text carefully – keep in mind that this is meant to be an article addressed to students. Make sure that you lead your readers in, keep them with you in clearly organised paragraphs, and send them off with a proper conclusion.

- Use information from the texts we have discussed in class, but also draw upon your own experience.
- In your article make use of <u>at least five of the performative verbs</u> listed below with <u>verb or clause complementation</u> (do not use noun complementation, please).
- <u>Underline</u> the verbs that you use in your text.

advise / allow / avoid / encourage / enjoy / (not) forget / get used to / insist / look forward to / mean / prevent / suggest / tell / refuse / regret / remember / stop / urge

5. Annotated Bibliography

Downing, A. (2005). *English Grammar: A University Course*. London: Tyler and Francis.
The second edition of an academic grammar which tries to relate syntax, semantics and pragmatics, taking a holistic approach; it caters mainly for advanced students of English who are not only interested in acquiring grammatical knowledge, but also need to use it for linguistic research purposes.

Gerngroß, G. and H. Puchta (1992). *Creative Grammar Practice*. Harlow: Longman.
The authors' approach to grammar is based on NLP models. The book offers very practical exercises and encourages learners to take a fresh look at traditional grammar.

Newby, D. (2003). *A Cognitive and Communicative Theory of Pedagogical Grammar*. Habilitationsschrift: Karl-Franzens Universität Graz.
In his thesis Newby combines cognitive linguistics with a pedagogical perspective in an innovative and cogent way, thus offering teachers a sound basis for teaching grammar.

Newby, D. (1991). *A Notional Grammar of Tense and Aspect*. Dissertation. Karl-Franzens Universität Graz.
Newby's notional approach to the English tense system provides

teachers with a very useful basis for teaching a grammar area that seems to be particularly difficult for German-speaking learners of English.

Reitbauer, M. and R. Vaupetitsch (2001). "Computergestützte Performanzanalyse von Lernerarbeiten". In: W. Börner and K. Vogel (2001). (eds.) *Grammatik Lehren und Lernen. Didaktisch-methodische und Unterrichtspraktische Aspekte.* Fremdsprachen in Lehre und Forschung 29. Bochum: AKS-Verlag. 137–152.

The authors show how to use learner corpora to design tailor-made course materials for intermediate to advanced learners.

Webliography

Townend, A. (2008). *English Grammar through Stories.* E book. [accessed 18.11.2008] http://www.english-test.net/pdf/samples/english-grammar-through-stories.pdf

Townend makes learners read specially designed stories that focus on particular grammar items and then makes them analyse those items. He takes the opposite approach to grammar stories as suggested in the present chapter.

Useful Links for using grammar stories on a lower level

http://www.english-test.net/pdf-worksheets/english-grammar-through-stories.html [accessed 18.11.2008]

http://www.rong-chang.com/qa2/stories/story001.htm [accessed 18.11.2008]

http://www.englishthroughstories.com/scripts/scripts.html [accessed 18.11.2008]

http://fremdsprachenundneuemedien.blogspot.com/2007/07/audio-for-eslefl-listen-and-read-along.html [accessed 18.11.2008]

3.3. A-I-D-A: From Text Analysis to Context-Sensitive Text Production

Margit Reitbauer and Renate Vaupetitsch

1. Rationale

Adult language users often want to and need to produce purpose-oriented effective texts. Such context-sensitive text production requires what Bloom (1956) calls higher order thinking skills, the ability to analyse and evaluate one's learning processes. Then, in order for texts to be effective, the writing must be monitored constantly by critical evaluation.

Many learners, however, only possess what Bloom (1956) calls lower order thinking skills, in other words, their foreign language acquisition has been mainly shaped by receptive and mechanistic learning processes. What these learners need is training in text analysis. They need some scaffolding that allows them to evaluate their own production critically and, as a next step, to then apply the conclusions that they draw from this analysis to their writing.

A-I-D-A is an acronym for a popular marketing strategy that was devised by John Caples in 1957:

A (raise Attention)
I (arouse Interest)
D (stimulate Desire)
A (provoke Action)

This strategy can be used as a tool for analysing the textual organisation of many purpose-oriented text types, e.g. letter of application, job offer, press release, various kinds of reports or reviews.

2. Procedure

Stage 1: Analyse

(1) Start with a target needs analysis: what text types do the learners need to produce and for what purposes; use the CEFR as a frame of reference for choosing a text type. (see example materials 1)
(2) Select model texts illustrating the text type chosen, and with the learners analyse and determine their generic features (see example materials 2).
(3) Use the A-I-D-A grid to specify the steps in text development (see example materials 3).
(4) Analyse the sections (A / I / ...) for lexico-grammatical features (recurrent syntactical patterns; recurrent vocabulary; typical cohesive devices). With some text types (e.g. letters) it is also important to draw learners' attention to layout conventions.

Stage 2: Draft

(5) Ask learners to write a first draft of their text.

Stage 3: Analyse

(6) Encourage peer-review and editing with the help of an A-I-D-A-grid-based editing sheet, ideally drawn up together with the learner-writers (see example material 4).
(7) Tell learners to conduct an individual needs analysis, followed by a discussion of the learning options open to the learner writers.

Stage 4: Produce

(8) Ask learners to produce the final version of their text.

3. Example materials

(1)

NEEDS ANALYSIS:
Based on an adaptation of CEFR descriptors for level C1 writing

	can do	need to learn
(1) I can express myself in writing on a wide range of general or professional topics in a clear and comprehensible way.	☐	☐
(2) I can present a complex topic in a clear and well structured way, highlighting the most important points, for example, in a composition or a report.	☐	☐
(3) I can present points of view in a comment on a topic or an event, underlining the main ideas and supporting my reasoning with detailed examples.	☐	☐
(4) I can put together information from different sources and relate it in a coherent summary.	☐	☐
(5) I can give a detailed description of experiences, feelings and events in a personal letter.	☐	☐
(6) I can write formally correct letters, for example, to complain or to take a stand in favour or against something.	☐	☐

(7) I can write a job application with CV.
☐ ☐

(8) I can write texts which show a high degree of grammatical correctness and vary my vocabulary and style according to the addressee, the kind of text and the topic.
☐ ☐

(9) I have a good command of complex sentence structures and can link parts of the text in a suitable way.
☐ ☐

(2)

Genre Analysis Form

Use the categories given below to analyse the texts and find their key characteristics. Give examples where possible for typical grammar structures or vocabulary used.

Communicative purpose (What does the writer hope to communicate/achieve?)
Expected audience (Who will read it?)
Layout (general *format* – e.g. does it have a title? What appears where on the page?)

Textual organisation (e.g. what type of information is included and in which order?)
Text-specific language Specific vocabulary/word partnerships Specific grammar

(3)

A-I-D-A GRID

OVERALL TEXTUAL ORGANISATION OF A LETTER OF APPLICATION

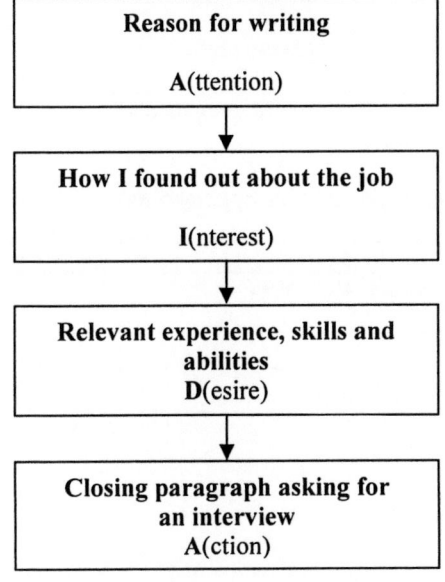

(4)

A-I-D-A EDITING
Letter of Application

		FEEDBACK	*Suggestions for changes*
Layout		Address / Date	
		Salutation/Valediction	
		Paragraph indication	
A-I-D-A			
Superstr.	A	The letter raises **attention** by	
	I	The letter arouses **interest** in the applicant by	
	D	The letter stimulates the **desire** to learn more about the applicant by	
	A	The letter provokes **action** by	
The 3 'a's'			
Language	a	Anything not **accurate**?	
	a	Range of structures and vocabulary **adequate**?	
	a	Register and tone **appropriate**?	
Comment		My personal comments:	

4. Possible variations

The A-I-D-A approach is particularly suitable for texts with a persuasive purpose; it could, however, be modified so that the focus is on conveying information or arguing a point.

5. Annotated bibliography

Caples, J. (1957). *Making Ads Pay*. New York: Dover Publications.
   This book is still a classic about print advertising by the man who is said to have created one of the most successful ads ever and on whose ideas the A-I-D-A scheme is based.
Hyland, K. (2003). *Second Language Writing*. Cambridge: Cambridge University Press.
   Hyland gives an up-to-date summary of the various approaches to teaching writing, including feedback strategies.
Tribble, C. (1996). *Writing*. Oxford: Oxford University Press.
   In this book Tribble applies the genre approach to the methodology of teaching learners how to write. This is an excellent book full of innovative ideas.

Webliography

Council of Europe (2001). Common European Framework of Reference for Languages: Learning, Teaching, Assessment. Strasbourg: Council of Europe.
   This text is also available at http://www.coe.int/T/DG4/Linguistic/ CADRE_EN.asp [accessed 17.12.2008]
http://www.mwp.hawaii.edu/resources/wm7.htm [accessed 15.12.2008]
   The University of Hawaii at Manoa offers advice to teachers of intensive writing courses on how to guide students towards effective peer reviewing. The page is based on the criteria lists that journal editors give to their reviewers. This is just one example of the many websites that deal with peer reviewing.

4. The *EAP* of Writing: *E*nhancing *A*cademic *P*roduction

Introduction to Section 4

Recent years have seen a tremendous increase in the number of EAP publications, so why produce yet more EAP materials? Our experience of teaching EAP to undergraduate students of English has led us to identify some problems which existing materials do not appear to address:

- Despite being taught how to paraphrase and summarise source material, students whose competence in written English is high still find it difficult to avoid plagiarism.
- Students experience difficulty in integrating what they have read with their own data and examples. As a result, students may abandon any attempt to include original input in their academic papers.
- Acquiring effective paraphrasing and summarising skills is only the first stage towards being able to produce an effective discussion of the relevant source literature. Students also need to learn how to synthesise different sources.
- Teaching approaches which focus exclusively on target texts (i.e. on product) can be detrimental to creating a text which really communicates content to the reader. Effective EAP teaching must emphasise in the first place the message the writer wants to communicate.

The first two chapters in this section (*Creative Use of Source Material* and *Producing a Synthesis of Academic Sources*) are complementary in that they address plagiarism in student papers as a skills issue rather a moral one. They assume that students have already acquired reasonable competence in written English and can paraphrase and summarise single sources fairly effectively. The first chapter demonstrates how students can be encouraged to use their own data to illustrate ideas from source texts while the second chapter demonstrates an interactive approach to teaching synthesising skills.

The third chapter in this section (*Improving the Readability of Students' Academic Writing*) focuses on academic register, specifically on the question of impersonality in academic texts. The author views taking a prescriptive approach to the creation of impersonal style (e.g. avoid 'I', use passive verbs rather than active) as potentially counterproductive because the resulting text may display odd information structure and thus be difficult to read. The chapter examines one of the main instruments used to create impersonality in an academic text – passive verbs – and encourages students to base their choice of active vs. passive verb on information structure.

The final chapter (*Writing an Abstract*) focuses on abstract writing. Students who wish to pursue academic study beyond undergraduate level need to be able to present their research in a concise and accessible manner. The ability to produce a well written abstract can in fact determine whether a conference or research proposal is accepted, and can therefore crucially affect the student's future academic career. The approach outlined in this chapter takes the actual research project as its starting point rather than the product, i.e. the abstract.

4.1. Creative Use of Source Material

Nancy Campbell

1. Rationale

Undergraduate students of foreign languages are often required to produce academic papers along the lines of a research article. All too often, these papers consist of barely disguised plagiarism, which students do not necessarily resort to because they are dishonest but because they lack confidence in their language skills. The temptation to plagiarise can be pre-empted by teaching students effective paraphrasing and summarising skills. Here it is important to provide students with practice material on synthesising several sources in addition to the single-source paraphrasing exercises provided in some English for Academic Purposes (EAP) course books (for example, McCormack and Slaght 2005; Manning 2008). Synthesising sources is the focus of Chapter 4.2 in the present volume.

However, acquisition of effective paraphrasing and summarising skills does not necessarily ensure that students produce papers which display any creative thinking. It is, of course, unrealistic to expect first year students to produce highly original research, but it is certainly desirable and realistic to expect them to produce more than a synopsis of other people's work. What students have to learn is how to integrate insights gained from reading relevant source material with their own examples.

To summarise, the teaching of extended academic writing should cover three skills:

- summarising and paraphrasing skills
- synthesising material from various sources
- integrating sources and original data/examples

The procedures suggested in this chapter focus on the third skill, namely, integrating sources and original data/examples.

2. Procedure

(1) Choose a topic for a seminar paper which relates to the students' academic course work, e.g. in literary studies or linguistics.
(2) Ask students to read an extract from an article or book relevant to the topic and to take notes. E.g. Yule, G. (1985/2006). *The Study of Language*. Cambridge: CUP. 114.
(3) Ask students to write a short summary of the extract. The first sentence should be a topic sentence, i.e. it should contain the main idea and a reference to the source.
(4) Discuss with the whole class which original examples could be used to illustrate ideas presented in the source text.
(5) Ask students to rewrite their summary, this time including their own examples (see example materials 3).
(6) Ask students to compare paragraphs in groups and choose the most successful texts to be discussed in class.

3. Example materials

(1) Seminar paper topic: "Texts are produced and received within a particular context." Take several texts and analyse the way in which context influences comprehension.
(2) Student summary without original examples

> Yule (2006: 114) defines the linguistic context or co-text of a word as the rest of the text which helps you to understand the meaning while the physical context refers to where and/or when you see or hear a word.

(3) Student summaries including original examples

> Yule (2006: 114) defines the linguistic context or co-text of a word as the rest of the text which helps you to understand the meaning while the physical context refers to where and/or when you see or hear a word. This can be illustrated by the word BAR. The sentences "Give me a bar of chocolate, please" and "We will

> have some drinks at this new bar tonight" both use the word BAR, but because of the surrounding words, we recognize the different meanings of the word and this is the linguistic context. An example for the physical context would be a building with the word BAR on it.

> Yule (2006: 114) defines the linguistic context or co-text of a word as the rest of the text which helps you to understand the meaning while the physical context refers to where and/or when you see or hear a word. If you take, for example, the word TRUST, it can have two different meanings. If you read it in a text along with words like confidence, faithfulness, commitment, relationship, it takes on a different meaning than if is accompanied by words like companies, fund etc. In this case the linguistic context determines the meaning. Concerning the physical context, you would know that trust relates to a group of companies if you see it written on a building whereas if you hear it from your partner in a personal conversation you know that he/she relies on you. The sentence "I trust in you" shows that both linguistic and physical context can together play a part in telling us the meaning of a word.

Commentary: Rather than simply reiterating Yule's example of the word BANK, the writers of the summaries above have discussed their own examples: BAR and TRUST. The writer of the second summary demonstrates that she is aware that there is not always a clear dividing line between linguistic and physical context when it comes to determining word meaning. This point is not made explicitly by Yule. The student's version therefore demonstrates her ability to think beyond the source text, and thus to work creatively with source material.

4. Possible variations

Step 3 of the procedure above can be omitted. Thus, the first draft of the summary would include the student's own examples.

5. Annotated bibliography

McCormack, J. and J. Slaght (2005). *English for Academic Study: Extended Writing and Research Skills*. Reading: Garnet Educational.
This book focuses on the writing process from planning an extended piece of academic writing to editing in preparation for submission, and includes a wealth of illustrative material from various academic disciplines.

Manning, A. (2008). *English for Language and Linguistics in Higher Eduction Studies*. Reading: Garnet Educational.
The book covers all four skills (reading, listening, speaking, writing) as well as vocabulary development, and the illustrative material is all derived from language and linguistics.

4.2. Producing a Synthesis of Academic Sources

Anja Burkert

1. Rationale

The importance of being able to synthesise ideas from various academic sources is recognised by the CEFR, which provides the following descriptor for writing at level B2: "Can synthesise information and arguments from a number of sources" (CEFR 2001: 62). However, although language learners at tertiary level may spend a considerable amount of time practising the skills of paraphrasing and summarising (see relevant sections in McCormack and Slaght 2005; Manning 2008), they seem to get practically no training in synthesising information from different academic sources. This may be partly due to the fact that this skill is largely ignored in published academic writing materials, an exception being Bailey (2006), who includes a 3-page section entitled *Combining Sources* in his academic writing handbook for international students.

The approach to synthesis presented in this chapter focuses on the strategies learners should use in order to synthesise information and arguments and integrates elements of a process approach to writing. To accomplish the task, learners will need prior training in paraphrasing and summarising and must be familiar with referencing conventions. From a linguistic and discoursal point of view, they will need a good command of the use of connectors and be able to contrast and compare different viewpoints. The suggested approach should prove motivating for learners because it employs authentic materials and has obvious relevance for learners' academic work. Further, working in groups should also promote learner independence.

2. Procedure

(1) The teacher selects 3–4 short authentic academic texts from books or journals dealing with a specific topic or topics relevant to the

learners' interests. (see example materials for some suggestions relevant for learners studying to become teachers).
(2) The teacher divides the class into groups of three or four people and gives each group three or four texts dealing with the same topic from different perspectives. Each member of the group receives a different text. All the groups can either work with the same set of texts or each group can be allocated a different topic.
(3) Working individually, each group member identifies the main points in his/her text and writes notes.
(4) Based on their written notes, each group member orally presents the information contained in their texts to the other members of their group.
(5) Together group members discuss and select the information from each text which they wish to include in a summary. One member of the group should take notes.
(6) Students consider the notes and delete/re-order information as appropriate.
(7) Collaboratively, the groups write a synthesis based on the revised notes. At this stage, learners could be provided with a sample synthesis. (see possible variations)
(8) The teacher then guides a whole class discussion of possible criteria for assessing syntheses such as appropriate referencing, clarity of meaning, grammatical accuracy. Together learners and teacher draw up a list of criteria and this is then displayed on an OHP.
(9) On the basis of these criteria the groups study each other's texts, review them and make suggestions for improvement.
(10) After the syntheses have been revised, they are 'published', i.e. made accessible to everybody, for example, by displaying them on the classroom walls.

3. Example materials

The following topics would be of interest to students aiming to become teachers. The list of sources is followed by a model summary.

Topic 1: Definitions of learner autonomy

Dam, L. (1995). *From Theory to Classroom Practice*. Dublin: Authentik. 1–2.
Holec, H. (1981). *Autonomy and Foreign Language Learning*. Oxford: Pergamon. 3–4.
Little, D.(1991). *Definitions, Issues and Problems*. Dublin: Authentik. 3–5.

Model summary

Holec (1981: 3) defines learner autonomy as the "ability to take charge of one's own learning". In doing so, Holec suggests that an autonomous learner must take "responsibility for all the decisions concerning all aspects of this learning", and he lists these decisions as follows:

- determining the objectives;
- defining the contents and progressions;
- selecting methods and techniques to be used;
- monitoring the procedure of acquisition properly speaking (rhythm, time, place, etc.);
- evaluating what has been acquired.

Holec clearly stresses that autonomy is a potential capacity and not a kind of behaviour and that this capacity is not inborn but must be acquired. Little (1991: 3–4), in contrast, considers multiple misconceptions surrounding the term and states that autonomy is not identical with self-instruction and certainly does not make the teacher redundant. Additionally, learner autonomy is not "something teachers do to their learners; in other words, (…) a new methodology" nor is it "a single, easily described behaviour". A further misconception according to Little is the assumption that autonomy is a permanent state achieved by certain learners. He points out that learners may show a great degree of autonomy in one area and be teacher-dependent in another one. Little (ibid: 4) finally offers his own definition of autonomy:

Essentially, autonomy is a capacity – for detachment, critical reflection, decision-making, and independent action. It presupposes, but also entails, that the learner will develop a particular kind of psychological relation to the process and content of his learning.

Although an autonomous learner enjoys a high degree of freedom, Little stresses the importance of the social aspect of learning. As social beings we are never totally independent but "our essential condition is one of interdependence" (ibid: 5).

Another definition which also emphasises the social dimension of learner autonomy is the definition offered by Bergen who sees the autonomous learner as "an active participant in the social processes of learning" (Bergen 1990: 102 as cited in Dam 1995: 1–2). This definition further stresses the *capacity* as well as *willingness* of learners to take responsibility for their own learning. Unlike Little (1991: 4), who points out that an autonomous learner may well be autonomous only in one specific area, the definition offered by Bergen states that an autonomous learner "can use this knowledge in any learning situation she/he may encounter at any stage in her/his life."

Topic 2: Origin of communicative language teaching

Brumfit, C. J. and K. Johnson, (eds.) (1979). *The Communicative Approach to Language Teaching.* Oxford: Oxford University Press. 3.
Howatt, A.P.R. (1984). *A History of English Language Teaching.* Oxford: Oxford University Press. 287.
Tudor, I. (1996). *Learner-centredness as Language Education.* Cambridge: Cambridge University Press. 7.

Model summary

Tudor (1996: 7) identifies two main motivations for the development of communicative language teaching: first, a widespread discontent with a code-based view of language teaching (e.g., the audio-lingual or grammar-translation method) and second, a wish to design language courses which should take the learners' real world communicative needs into account. Dissatisfaction with the traditional view of language is also identified by Brumfit and Johnson (1979: 3), who see communicative language teaching as "a reaction against the view of language as a set of structures"; CLT views language as communication and puts meaning and use of language at the forefront. Howard (1984: 287) makes a similar observation stating that structural syllabuses, materials, and methods were widely felt to be inadequate for learners' real world communication needs. Instead, it was perceived as being crucial to put language *use* before language *form* and provide learners with practical skills to communicate in the foreign language.

Topic 3: Definitions of teacher development

Head, K. and P. Taylor (1997). *Reading in Teacher Development*. Oxford: Macmillan Heinemann.1.
Lange, D. (1990). "A blueprint for a teacher development program". In: J. C. Richards and D. Nunan (eds). *Second Language Teacher Education*. NY: Cambridge University Press. 250.
Underhill, A. (1997). "Preface." In: K. Head and P. Taylor (eds.) *Reading in Teacher Development*. Oxford: Macmillan Heinemann. vii.

Model summary

Head and Taylor (1997: 1) see teacher development as complementary to teacher training, which is dominated by an external agenda. Teacher development, in contrast, primarily means being willing and able to change and to improve one's teaching practice through self-awareness and reflection. Thus, the motivation for teacher development and also the potential for change are to be found internally within teachers themselves. Underhill (1997: vii) defines teacher development as "the process of becoming the best teacher you can be" by oneself becoming a student of learning. As he points out, the process of developing as a teacher is never finished. Indeed, Lange's definition of teacher development contrasts it with teacher training and preparation and stresses the continual, long-term perspectives.

Teacher development is used in the literature to describe a process of continual intellectual, experiential, and attitudinal growth of teachers (...). I have argued for the use of the term, distinguishing it from training and preparation as encompassing more and allowing for continued growth both before and throughout a career (...) Lange (1990: 250)

Topic 4: Differences between teacher training and teacher development

Bailey, K. M., A. Curtis and D. Nunan (2001). *Pursuing Professional Development: The Self as Source.* Boston: Heinle and Heinle. 6–8.
Wallace, M. (1998). *Action Research for Language Teachers.* Cambridge: Cambridge University Press. 6.
Woodward, T. (1991). *Models and Metaphors In Language Teacher Training: Loop Input and Other Strategies.* New York: Cambridge University Press. 146–147.

Model summary

Woodward (1991: 146–147) offers a list of characteristic features of both teacher development and teacher education. She contrasts various features of the two, such as the voluntary element in teacher development versus the compulsory one in teacher education, the long-term versus short-term aspect, the internal versus the external agenda, and the fact that teacher development is done with peers as opposed to teacher education, which is done with experts. In terms of the reasons why teachers choose to engage in teacher development, Bailey et al. (2001: 6–7) offer various suggestions: to acquire new knowledge and skills, to stay abreast of developments in the field, to potentially increase income and prestige, to lead to personal empowerment and fight negativity in their teaching lives. Wallace (1998: 10) sees teachers' self-esteem as a prerequisite for undertaking professional activities and explains that professional development of teachers is "a rational and intrinsic part of the good professional's life":

Self-awareness of potential areas of improvement is therefore helpful provided it goes along with a reasonably good self-image. The leap into the unknown is unlikely to take place unless it can be done from a secure and stable platform of self-esteem (ibid: 6).

4. Possible variations

You could take a top-down approach and start by using model texts. Before producing their own syntheses, learners could be presented with a sample synthesis. Learners could be encouraged to analyse the synthesis in relation to different aspects such as conventions of referring to source, direct quotations and paraphrases, academic register, use of connectors, clarity and relevance of information. After having been presented with a sample synthesis, learners should advance to producing their own syntheses as described above.

5. Annotated bibliography

Bailey, S. (2006). *Academic Writing: A Handbook for International Students*. London: Routledge.
This handbook is aimed at international students who have to write exams or coursework in English.

Council of Europe (2001). *Common European Framework of Reference for Languages: Learning, Teaching, Assessment.* Strasbourg: Council of Europe.
This text is also available at http://www.coe.int/T/DG4/Linguistic/ CADRE_EN.asp [accessed 17.12.2008]

McCormack, J. and J. Slaght (2005). *English for Academic Study: Extended Writing and Research Skills.* Reading: Garnet Educational.
This book focuses on the writing process from planning an extended piece of academic writing to editing in preparation for submission, and includes a wealth of illustrative material from various academic disciplines.

Manning, A. (2008). *English for Language and Linguistics in Higher Education Studies.* Reading: Garnet Educational.
This book covers all four skills (reading, listening, speaking, writing) as well as vocabulary development. The illustrative material is all derived from language and linguistics.

4.3. Improving the Readability of Students' Academic Writing

Nancy Campbell

1. Rationale

Teachers at tertiary level will be all too familiar with student writing which displays surface cohesion in the form of appropriate use of connectors and other cohesive devices, but is still difficult to read. The reason for this impression of poor readability often lies in the text failing to conform to acceptable patterns of information structure in English, which may differ greatly from patterns familiar to students from their first language (see Brown and Yule 1983: 5.2; Halliday and Hasan 1976: 7.4.1,). The importance of information structure is highlighted in the Common European Framework of Reference (5.2.3.1), which specifically mentions the distribution of given/new information in texts as an essential aspect of discourse competence. The problem of readability is also addressed in the extended CEFR descriptors for C1 (top band) and C2 produced by the Austrian ELTT group[1], which state that texts should "not put too much strain on the reader".

This chapter focuses on one aspect of academic register, the use of passive verbs, and suggests an approach which encourages students to consider choice of active versus passive verbs in terms of appropriate information structure rather than simply in terms of academic register. This approach assumes that students are familiar with the concept of cohesion and coherence and are at least aware of the function of lexis and conjunctives in creating cohesion. However, it does not assume any awareness of information structure patterns in English. It should be stressed that this approach uses a simplified notion of information structure, but this is justified by students' general lack of familiarity with this aspect of text.

---

[1] The Austrian ELTT (English Language Teaching and Testing) group consists of university teachers of language and linguistics whose aim is to establish exit levels in language competence for BA graduates in English Studies. The ELTT rating scale for writing and benchmarked sample texts can be accessed at http://www.uni-klu.ac.at/ltc/inhalt/430.htm.

When using the procedures suggested in this chapter, teachers might find it necessary to present a considerable quantity of illustrative material in class.

2. Procedure

(1) Introduce students to three key aspects of information structure in English (discussed in example materials 1).
(2) Select a text or text extract written by a student which displays awkward use of passive verbs, but does not have any obvious lexical and grammatical errors. It may be necessary to correct any lexical and grammatical errors beforehand in order to avoid detracting the students' focus from information structure (see example materials 2).
(3) Ask students to comment on the text. It may be the case that students are fairly satisfied with the text because it does not have obvious language errors. The teacher can provide input on information structure errors (see example materials 3).
(4) Present students with a rewritten version of the text which displays more acceptable patterns of information structure. Students should identify what has been altered in the original text and try to give reasons (see example materials 4).
(5) Set a writing task (see example materials 5). Using the OHP, board or computer, the class writes a text together with teacher assistance.

- Teacher writes up a topic sentence.
- Class discusses the focus of the sentence and ways in which this focus can be referred to in the next sentence.
- Students formulate and write up sentence 2.
- Class discusses possible sentences and selects the most suitable. The teacher adds the chosen sentence to the topic sentence.
- Teacher and students continue this procedure to produce a paragraph of 5–6 sentences.

(6) Students move on to group or individual writing. They repeat step 5 either in groups or individually. Before submitting the paragraph, they should mark the given and new information in the text in different colours.

3. Example materials

(1) Key aspects of information structure

- The strongest part of a sentence is the predicate. Consider, for example, possible contexts for these sentences (also discussed in Grellet 1983: 129):

I saw Jane last Friday

It was on Friday that I saw Jane.

The focus of the second example is "on Friday", which leads us to assume a situation in which the speaker wishes to clarify the precise day of the encounter with Jane.

- Texts are normally constructed according to the principle *given....new*. New information in one sentence becomes given information in the next.

I broke my leg last week. This was why I had to cancel my holiday.

- The decision to use an active or a passive verb should be based in the first place on the requirements of information structure, not register. Impersonality can also be created through using nouns: for example, the sentence

If you fail your exam, you won't be allowed to attend the next course.

can be rendered as

Students who fail the exam cannot attend the next course.

or

Failure in the exam precludes students from attending the next course.

whereby the lexical choice in the second sentence (e.g. precludes) makes it more formal.

The alternative using the passive

If the exam is failed, the next course cannot be attended.

appears rather awkward because the main focus of each clause has largely been expressed in subject position (the exam, the next course), thus violating given/new information structure:

(2) Use of passive or active verbs

Discuss the use of passive verbs in the following introduction to a seminar paper written by a student[2]. Which ones are appropriate and which should be changed?

> *Protoptypes and prototype theory have been the subject of linguistic and psychological studies since the 1970s. Well-known researchers, such as Eleanor Rosch, have dedicated their research to this field of linguistics, achieving interesting insights. However, prototype theory has also been criticised due to various shortcomings.*
>
> *The topic of this seminar paper is not prototypes themselves but more whether they are culturally determined. This means that, on the basis of GOE ratings (Goodness of Exemplar – see p.4), prototypes of specific categories can be established. GOE ratings from international research will be compared to one another and possible cultural differences will be discussed in order to explore the influence of culture on prototypes.*
>
> *Firstly, basic information about prototypes and prototype theory will be given. Secondly, the methodology of the research for this paper will be outlined by describing the modus operandi of GOE ratings more closely and after that a discussion of the results of the question-*

---

[2] Proseminar paper written for a university class in Semantics in Summer Semester 2008 by a second year Austrian student.

> naire will follow. To conclude, the findings of the research will be reviewed.

(3) Teacher input

Paragraph one (my underlining)

> Protoptypes and prototype theory have been <u>the subject of linguistic and psychological studies since the 1970s</u>. Well-known researchers, such as Eleanor Rosch, have <u>dedicated their research to this field of linguistics, achieving interesting insights</u>. However, prototype theory has <u>also been criticised due to various shortcomings</u>.

This paragraph is fine as it stands. The sentences all place the most important information in predicate position (underlined) and therefore it is not necessary to change any of the verb phrases. "Various shortcomings" should perhaps have been developed more fully but the following paragraph does state that the paper will critically examine one aspect of prototype theory, i.e. whether prototypes are culturally determined, and this implies that the paper will explore a potential shortcoming of existent research on prototypes.

Paragraph two (my underlining)

> The topic of this seminar paper is not prototypes themselves but more whether they are culturally determined. This means that, on the basis of GOE ratings (Goodness of Exemplar – see p.4), prototypes of specific categories <u>can be established</u>. GOE ratings from international research <u>will be compared</u> to one another and possible cultural differences <u>will be discussed</u> in order to explore the influence of culture on prototypes.

The second sentence has a long subject and a very short predicate consisting of a verb phrase alone, which breaks a norm of information structure. There is no clear motivation for the passives in the third sentence, except to create an impersonal style. A further problem is the lack of cohesion between sentences one and two: what does "this" at the beginning of sentence two refer to? Further, introducing GOE ratings at this stage without further explanation does not make sense to the uninitiated reader.

Paragraph three

> *Firstly, basic information about prototypes and prototype theory will be given. Secondly, the methodology of the research for this paper will be outlined by describing the modus operandi of GOE ratings more closely and after that a discussion of the results of the questionnaire will follow. To conclude, the findings of the research will be reviewed.*

The use of the first person pronoun 'I' in an academic paper is more a question of personal taste rather than of acceptable register. I see no reason why 'I' should not be used at least in the Introduction. The use of the passives in the student's original version creates unwieldy sentences with long subjects, short predicates and a resulting odd information structure.

(4) Rewritten version

> *Protoptypes and prototype theory have been the subject of linguistic and psychological studies since the 1970s. Well-known researchers, such as Eleanor Rosch, have dedicated their research to this field of linguistics, achieving interesting insights. However, prototype theory has also been criticised due to various shortcomings.*
>
> *The topic of this seminar paper is not prototypes themselves but more whether they are culturally determined. If they are, this would mean it is possible to establish prototypes of specific categories of experience. I will compare GOE (Goodness of Exemplar – see p.4) ratings from international research to one another and discuss possible cultural differences in order to discover the influence of culture on prototypes.*
>
> *Firstly, I will present basic information about prototypes and prototype theory. Secondly, I will outline my research methodology by describing the modus operandi of GOE ratings more closely and then*

> *discuss the results of my questionnaire. Finally, I will review my findings.*

The third paragraph could also be rendered as follows, thus avoiding 'I'.

> *The first section of the paper will present basic information about prototypes and prototype theory while the second section outlines my research methodology by describing the modus operandi of GOE ratings more closely. The third section discusses the results of my questionnaire and the final section reviews my findings.*

(5) Writing task for whole class, group and individual writing[3].

Identify the focus of the topic sentence and write an appropriate second sentence. Repeat this procedure to produce a paragraph of 5–6 sentences.

Topic sentence: *Many students suffer from anxiety when they are faced with their first university exam.*

The paragraph could develop in <u>one</u> of these directions:

- Outlining some **reasons** why students feel anxious about their first exams
- Giving **advice** on what can be done to counteract anxiety
- Describing some of the physical and psychological **symptoms** of anxiety

4. Possible variations

Students produce rewritten versions themselves.

---

[3] Tasks devised by Jennifer Schumm and Nancy Campbell for an EAP class for first semester students of English. These tasks deliberately do not focus on a specific subject area (e.g. linguistics, literature, cultural studies) in order to avoid students having to possess specialist knowledge.

5. Annotated bibliography

Brown, G. and G. Yule (1983). *Discourse Analysis.* Cambridge: Cambridge University Press.
Chapter 5 contains a comprehensive account of information structure in spoken and written texts.
Council of Europe (2001). *Common European Framework of Reference for Languages: Learning, Teaching, Assessment.* Strasbourg: Council of Europe.
This text is also available at http://www.coe.int/T/DG4/Linguistic/CADRE_EN.asp [accessed 17.12.2008]
Grellet, F.(1981). *Developing Reading Skills.* Cambridge: Cambridge University Press.
Chapter 3 (Thematization) includes useful exercises to raise learners' awareness of information structure.
Halliday, M .A .K and R. Hasan (1976). *Cohesion in English.* London: Longman.
This book is still the most comprehensive account of the topic.

Webliography

ELTT rating scale for writing. http://www.uni-klu.ac.at/ltc/inhalt/430.htm [accessed 29. 12. 2008].
The website includes benchmarked sample texts.

4.4. Writing an Abstract

Ulla Fürstenberg

1. Rationale

An abstract is a short, concise text structured according to precise rules. It lends itself particularly well to peer-correction and re-writing since it is usually intended for publication in some form, and therefore must achieve a high degree of perfection.

To write a successful abstract, students must think about text production in terms of the communication process. They need to develop an awareness of the importance of logical structure in helping readers to understand the most significant points of their texts. Additionally, to communicate effectively on complex issues, they need to be able to express themselves clearly in a style that is appropriate to the text type.

In the learner-centered approach presented in this chapter, the complex task of writing an abstract is broken down into smaller steps. In a first step, students are encouraged to talk about their research projects using informal language, which allows them to concentrate fully on the content and the key points they wish to make in their abstracts before they attempt to structure their ideas and to express them in more formal academic language.

2. Procedure

(1) Hand out Worksheet 1 and give students 10–15 minutes to think about the four questions and make notes. They then work in pairs and tell each other about their projects. (see example materials 1).

(2) In an open discussion with the whole group, encourage students to discuss their answers to the four questions. In these first two steps, they use informal language to talk about their work.

(3) Hand out Worksheet 2 (see example materials 2). Explain that the four questions on Worksheet 1 correspond to four of the five essential elements of an abstract on Worksheet 2. Ask students to match

up the questions to the appropriate element as illustrated in the table in example materials 3.
(4) Choose published abstracts from a field that is of interest to the students. Students should read these abstracts and identify the essential elements of an abstract which are listed in Worksheet 2 (see example materials 2).
(5) Discuss the following questions with the students: What are the characteristics of an abstract? Who is the intended reader?
(6) Hand out Worksheet 3 (see example materials 4). Explain that the essential elements of an abstract are marked in the text by highly formulaic language. Students should extend the list of useful phrases on the worksheet by adding examples of appropriate language from the abstracts they have analyzed.
(7) Explain that for 'Background', an introductory sentence that briefly places their research project in context is usually sufficient. The students now have a framework and some essential language elements for writing a first draft of their own abstract (homework).
(8) In class, ask students to give peer feedback: students swap abstracts, read a fellow student's abstract and comment on the following points:

- Does the abstract contain all the essential elements?
- Is it reader-friendly? Is it appropriate for the intended reader?
- Is the language appropriate to the text type?

(9) Ask students to produce a second draft of their abstracts. This version is read and corrected by the teacher.

3. Example materials

(1) Worksheet 1: TALKING ABOUT YOUR RESEARCH

WHY are you doing your study / project?

WHAT are you investigating, and HOW?

WHAT are your findings so far?

WHAT do your findings mean?

(2) Worksheet 2

(Adapted from:
http://www.olemiss.edu/depts/writing_center/grabstract.html)
[accessed 29.12.08]

Essential elements of the abstract are:

- **Background:** A simple opening sentence or two placing the work in context.
- **Aims:** One or two sentences giving the purpose of the work.
- **Method(s):** One or two sentences explaining what was done. (Described at length only if it is unusual)
- **Results:** One or two sentences indicating the main findings. (Absolutely essential)
- **Conclusions:** One sentence giving the most important consequence of the work. (Telling what the results mean).

An abstract should include the few things you would like your reader to remember long after the details of your paper may be forgotten.

(3) Table

Worksheet 1: Questions	Worksheet 2: 'Essential Elements'
	Background
Why are you doing your study / project?	Aims
What are you investigating, and how?	Method(s)
What are your findings so far?	Results
What do your findings mean?	Conclusions

(4) Worksheet 3

Useful Phrases for Abstracts

Aims / Objectives

The purpose of this thesis/study is to show …
         to find out …
 This thesis examines …
         assesses …
         evaluates …
         investigates …
 This thesis deals with …
         focuses on …
         aims at …
 The aim/objective of this thesis is to …

Methods

Research is based on …
 Different types of …. are reviewed.
 The theoretical/practical section gives an insight into …
         gives an overview of …
         is based on …

Interpreting Data, Describing Results
These findings indicate that ...   show that ... These results provide evidence of ... This research shows that ... This research provides some evidence that ... This thesis demonstrates that ...
Explaining Conclusions
The implications of these findings are... We can conclude from the survey that... We can draw the following conclusions from these results...

(4) Sample student abstract

[BACKGROUND] *Experts in the Austrian province of Styria have demonstrated that people who are undergoing a substitute treatment programme have fewer chances on the labour market. Even jobs in sheltered workplaces are more difficult to obtain for this group.* [AIMS] *This thesis investigates the reasons for this exclusion and shows what options exist for this group.* [METHODS] *Research is based on qualitative interviews with experts who work in facilities and projects that provide sheltered workplaces. Furthermore, the practical part of the thesis gives an overview of such projects and organisations in Styria.* [RESULTS] *Research carried out for this thesis provides evidence that participants of substitute treatment programmes are not penalised because of the programme as such, but rather because of physical and mental issues caused by their addiction.* [CONCLUSIONS] *Providing more sheltered workplaces with a very low threshold of access could create more opportunities for people who are unable to cope with the demands of the regular labour market.*

4. Possible variations

- Step 4 can be completed before Step 3. Thus, students would try to analyze the structure of an abstract without prior knowledge of the five essential elements.
- The same procedure could be used for other highly formalized text types, e.g. letters of application.
- Step 8 (peer feedback) could be carried out by e-mail or on a learning platform to save classroom time and provide additional writing practice.

5. Annotated bibliography

Bailey, S. (2006). *Academic Writing: A Handbook for International Students.* 2nd ed. London: Routledge.
If students have trouble identifying the main points of their thesis, *Academic Writing* has a chapter on "Selecting Key Points" that could be used for practice.

Hamp-Lyons, L. and B. Heasley (2006). *Study Writing: A Course in Writing Skills for Academic Purposes.* 2nd ed. Cambridge: Cambridge University Press.
This course book has a strong focus on peer feedback in the writing process. It also includes advice on how to work with a virtual peer group.

McCarthy, M. and F. O'Dell (2008). *Academic Vocabulary in Use.* Cambridge: Cambridge University Press.
The procedure described in this chapter assumes that students are already familiar with the academic language they need to write their abstracts. If they need more input, *Academic Vocabulary in Use* is a useful resource, especially the sections on "Opinions and Ideas" and "Functions".

5. Genre Switching

Introduction to Section 5

This section focuses on the role of genre in effective and appropriate text production at advanced level. Many learners have difficulties in writing freely, even at advanced tertiary level, and often need support and structured frameworks in order to enhance their confidence in writing. In particular, learners seem to lack an awareness of the range of factors which contribute towards successful, purposeful written communication across contexts. The authors in this section report on approaches which examine the conventions of various genres. They describe a series of tasks which are structured in order to support learners in their attempt to produce texts which employ these genre characteristics.

In the first chapter (*Using Literature for Genre Switching*), the author explores two literary genres, the short story and the ballad. In this approach, learners are encouraged to engage with the texts on both a macro- and micro-level, considering overall effects and mood but also focusing on linguistic details and choices. In this way, learners consider the text both as a literary work and as a linguistic product. Learners are guided through a series of activities to their own text production in the form of genre switching. Finally, learners transform one text of a particular genre (short story) into another genre (ballad), following genre conventions established in the analytical stages but retaining the content and mood from the original text type.

In the second chapter in this section (*Popular Songs: Text in(to) Song – Song in(to) Text*), the potential of song is considered for language teaching purposes. The author shows how songs can be used to help learners examine various aspects of language such as semantic, lexis, register etc. and how they can be used in English for Specific Purposes (ESP) settings. Certain songs, such as the Bob Dylan song examined in this chapter, are well-suited to developing learners' awareness of narrative structure, form and content. The author suggests a series of activities designed to help learners recognise core narrative elements and appreciate how narratives can be differently represented across genres and communicative contexts.

The final chapter (*Transferring Content across Genres*) examines one particularly predictable genre, recipes, in order to help learners become aware of the nature and role of genre in text production. In the analytical approach to genre outlined in this chapter, learners develop a metacognitive awareness of text conventions and are then asked to transfer content from a narrative, to the genre analysed, recipe. This approach ultimately encourages creative text production.

5.1. Using Literature for Genre-Switching

Ingrid Pfandl-Buchegger

1. Rationale

Although language learning and literary studies are often seen as two separate domains within the university curriculum, literary texts can enrich the repertoire of language teaching materials by offering carefully designed, well-structured texts which employ sophisticated rhetorical structures. Literary texts can be used to raise learners' awareness of genre conventions as well as the potential of emotional expression offered by the strategic use of language. Additionally, literary texts are able to provide a valuable insight into the cultural and historical background of a language community although this is an aspect not explored specifically in these activities.

The following activities are intended to raise learners' awareness of literary genre conventions and sensitize them to the characteristics of various text types and the subtle differences that can be created by using different literary genres, both on the level of the **story** (selection of events) and its presentation. They offer learners the chance to explore the role of genre conventions, the effects of language choices and other aspects of presentation, as well as the overall emotional effect of text. In this way, literature can help to fine-tune advanced learners' skills in the subtleties of language use, raise their awareness of perception mechanisms and genre conventions and also improve their understanding of the impact of a text on the reader. Finally, the form of peer teaching and active learning employed in these activities helps learners to engage with the texts and their structure on a deeper level.

Ballads, one of the genre chosen for this chapter, are popular with students and are suitable for language teaching given their relatively simple, natural, everyday language and straight-forward, uncomplicated rhythm. The other genre, the short story, can be put to good use in language teaching given that they tend to contain all the key elements of a narrative, a single strand of action and individualized characters. These features make them ideally suited as a model to be emulated by language learners when constructing their own narratives.

2. Procedure

(1) In preparation: Before the next class, learners are asked to read a short story and a ballad. Examples used in this article which have worked well in the past: Truman Capote, "Miriam", and W. H. Auden's ballad, "Miss Gee". Both texts share the common themes of old age, loneliness and isolation.
Whilst reading, the learners should prepare any unknown vocabulary and complete a table summarising each text (see example materials 1). If necessary, a glossary of key words could be handed out with the texts.

(2) In class: Divide the class into groups of 6 learners and seat them at 'islands' of tables. Explain that one half of the group (i.e., 3 of the students) are going to 'specialise' on the story and the other half on the ballad. They will then peer teach each other about their specialist text throughout the session and in so doing, learn about both text types.
Ask one half of each group to summarize the content of the story, the other half to summarize the content of the ballad by comparing the tables they completed for homework. They should also discuss their personal reactions to the texts (see example materials 2 for more detailed possible questions).
Then they should share their findings and discuss their respective text type with the other half of the group, so that all 6 students have the opportunity to consider both text types.

(3) The teacher can then explain to the whole class that ballads were originally sung and have a strong affinity to music. Each group should therefore collectively choose and decide upon a tune that they feel fits the mood and atmosphere of the text.

(4) Groups report back to the whole class on their discussions, including their choice of tune and reasons for their choice, as well as their personal responses to the texts.

(5) Learners listen to the actual tune the author had in mind when composing the ballad and are invited to comment on the impact of the

music on the mood and any possible changes to their perception of the message of the ballad text. Learners should also reflect on and compare the effects of the actual tune with their choice of music. (see additional information on critical reactions to Auden's ballad).

(6) Having now discussed the texts at a macro-level in terms of content and the learners' personal reactions to them, the groups are then given a second table to complete which focuses on each text type in more detail. (see example materials 3). (see example materials 4 for one possible example of how to complete the table with these text types taking a more literary focus).

To begin with, each 'specialist' half of the group of 6 should focus on completing their table for their particular text type only. Then each specialist group takes it in turn to 'teach' the other half about their text type. The learners are asked to not only share their answers to the table but to illustrate and show the other half of the group how they analysed the text using examples from the text. The learners are encouraged to ask questions and work together to find any additional elements not identified by the specialists. Ultimately, each group should have fully completed tables about both text types.

(7) The teacher then elicits answers for the table from the whole class about what the constituent features of each text type are. This table is completed on an OHP with any necessary additions from the teacher.

(8) Again in their groups, the learners are asked to now switch the ballad into a short story or the short story into a ballad. Depending on the confidence and level of the learners, students can be asked to switch *into* their 'specialist' text type or *out of* it. It is useful to encourage students to transform from their 'specialist' text type into the other one to ensure they have fully grasped the characteristics of the other text type which they have not examined in such detail. The learners should use the framework from the analysis stages 6 and 7 to help ensure they maintain the genre characteristics.

(9) Before they begin writing, learners will need to discuss the changes that need to be effected (e.g., length, selection of events, change of voice/perspective, language etc.) to switch across genres and should prepare an outline together.

Students then actually write their ballad/story following the conventions and making any necessary changes.

(10) When they are finished, they exchange texts with the other half of their group who, as the specialists, evaluate how well their peers have adhered to the text conventions of their specialist genre. All the finished versions of the two text types are displayed in class for learners to walk around and read. It is also possible to then hold a final discussion for the whole class to talk about the task, what they have learned from the experience and the role of genre conventions generally.

3. Example materials

(1) Table summarising both texts. To be completed by learners in preparation for the class:

Short Story: "Miriam"	**Ballad: "Miss Gee"**
Who	Who
What	What
When	When
Where	Where
Personal reaction to the text	Personal reaction to the text

(2) Possible detailed questions about learners' personal responses to the texts:

a. How do you like the text as a whole?
b. How does it make you feel?
c. What in the text affects you? (e.g., topic, language, rhythm etc.) In what ways?
d. What image/character/section of text is most powerful for you and why?
e. Why do you think the author has chosen the particular form (ballad or short story) for this subject?

(3) Second table to analyse texts at a micro-level:

	Short Story	**Ballad**
Length & layout		
Content elements & sequence of events		
Structure		
Point of view/ perspective		
Language: Time markers		
Language: Descriptive/ emotive language		
Language: Syntax		
Language: Rhythm and sound effects		

(4) Example of possible characteristics of short story and ballad:

Characteristics of short story based on 'Miriam'
Short Story: **Length & layout:**   Short narrative text, written in prose   **Content elements & sequence of events:**   focus on one single theme or strand of action   narrated in the past tense/preterite   straight chronological order, begins with a general description of Mrs. Miller's life and habits (first paragraph), then focuses on individual events (*Then she met Miriam.*) or   e.g. *It snowed all week* (general) … *That evening she scrambled* … (specific event)   individualized characters, realistic detail   **Structure:**   logical structure, tightly knit plot (beginning, turning point, end)   **Point-of-view/perspective**:   External narrator, third-person narrator   focus on the perceptions, feelings and thoughts of the main character   invites empathy and identification with the main character (sharing her thoughts and fears)   **Language:**   **Time Markers:**   Starts with summary narration (see first paragraph: *for several years, never, rarely, seldom, occasional*), then continues with specific time and place, sequence: *Then she met Miriam* (see also: *that night, that evening, then, at first, the next day, at precisely five*, etc.)   **Descriptive/emotive language:**   use of highly symbolic and figurative language in the descriptive passages, many adjectives   e.g.   *description of the snow: *deadening, hushing, soundlessly, secretly*

*description of Miriam:
> *She was thin and fragilely constructed;*
> *her hair was the longest and strangest Mrs. Miller had ever seen;*
> *a simple, special elegance;*
> *gracefully;*
> *her fingers gracefully and musical-looking*

*description of Mrs Miller's feelings: *Mrs Miller felt oddly excited*
*images (unreal, dream-like atmosphere)
e.g. *angrily; like a flower in bloom; desperate; passionate*, etc.
*similes: *oblivious as a mole burrowing a blind path*

Syntax:
complex sentence structure, mirrors Mrs Miller's habits and character: matter-of-fact, well-ordered, straightforward narrative of action (see first paragraph)

Rhythm and sound effects:
prose, no obvious rhythm (though the language is very 'poetical' through the use of images and symbols)

Characteristics of ballad based on 'Miss Gee'

Ballad:
Length & layout:
Poem, written in stanzas (of 4 lines)
Metre: regular metrical pattern
('ballad stanza': alternating lines of 4 feet and 3 feet, i.e. 4 and 3 stresses with an unfixed number of unstressed syllables per line)
but: Auden here uses a simplified pattern of only 3 stress lines that emphasizes the monotony of Miss Gee's life
e.g. *Let me tell you a little story / About Miss Edith Gee*
    x x x' x x x' x x' x / x x' x   x' x x'
    She lived in Clevendon Terrace/ At number 83(eighty-three)
    x   x'   x x' x   x x' x / x x' x   x' x   x'
Rhyme: lines 1 and 3 rhyme (*Gee – three, small – all*)

Content elements & sequence of events:
Ballads combine lyrical (rhythm, rhyme, sound structure), dramatic (dialogue) and narrative elements (tells a story: see l. 1 *Let me tell you a little story*)

Combination of general and specific elements:
Begins with general elements (description of Miss Gee and presentation of her repetitive every-day life),
then continues with specific detail/events (story elements = chronological sequence of selected individual scenes – *dream, visit to the doctor, operation* –, presented in great detail, often using dialogue)

Structure:
No connectors or time markers, often logical and time gaps (between stanzas, e.g. stanzas 5/6, 9/10 etc.)
e.g.
 They lay her on the table,
  The students began to laugh;
 And Mr. Rose the surgeon
  He cut Miss Gee in half.
Repetition of elements (habitual action and summary)
e.g.
 She passed the loving couples/ She turned her head away
 She passed the loving couples/ And they didn't ask her to stay.
 The days and nights went by her/ Like waves round a Cornish wreck
 She bicycled to the evening service
 She bicycled down to the doctor

Point-of-view/perspective:
Impersonal voice/speaker (e.g. *Let me tell you a little story*),
outside view of the characters (no thought presentation),
pseudo-objective: no explicit comments or value judgements (straightforward rendering of action and dialogue),
does not invite empathy or identification with a character

Language:
Time markers: very few time markers, unspecific and generalized in the summaries
e.g. *The days and nights went by her; Summer made the trees a picture/Winter made them a wreck*
specific in the individual scenes (*one evening*)

Descriptive/emotive language:
extremely sober, blunt and unemotional descriptions of main character's exterior and actions (few adjectives), but creating an implicit commentary through repetition, parallelisms, and negative connotations of words
e.g.
> *She had a slight squint in her left eye*
> *Her lips they were thin and small*
> *She had narrow sloping shoulders*
> *And she had no bust at all.*
>
> *She bicycled to the evening service*
>   *With her clothes buttoned up to her neck. ...*
> *She bicycled down to the doctor*
>   *With her clothes buttoned up to her neck. ...*
> *[She] Lay in the ward for women*
>   *With her bedclothes right up to her neck*
>
> *They hung her from the ceiling*
>   *Yes, they hung up Miss Gee;*

Irony through incongruous use of speech and over-simplification
e.g.
> *'Lead me not into temptation*
>   *But make me a good girl, please.'*

Syntax:
very simple sentence structure (colloquial language), paratactic (*and*), repetitive, very few connectives
e.g.
> *She'd a purple mac for wet days,*
>   *A green umbrella too to take,*
> *She'd a bicycle with a shopping basket*
>   *And a harsh back-pedal break.*

Emphatic use of the pronoun (in imitation of Black English)
> *And Mr. Rose the surgeon*
>   *He cut Miss Gee in half.*

> **Rhythm and sound effects**:
> rhythmical, but simple straightforward everyday language, repetition of sounds, words, phrases
> e.g.
> *She did a lot of knitting/ Knitting for the Church Bazaar;*
> *Miss Gee knelt down in the side-aisle/ She knelt down on her knees*
> *They hung her from the ceiling/ Yes, they hung up Miss Gee;*

4. Possible variations

- For a shorter activity, all the learners just transfer from one genre to the other together (e.g., short story into ballad). Equally, for a longer activity, learners can be asked to do both.
- Learners can perform their final transferred texts.
- Learners can be asked to write a short story or ballad of their choice following the conventions but without a base text to switch from.
- Students can be asked to bring their favourite pop ballads and short stories on a topic and use these materials rather than teacher-selected texts – especially if you have advanced learners and maybe wish to discuss genre variation.
- Other genres can be used to those suggested here. In this example, we used ballads and short stories but other literary genres could be used such as short stories, poems, etc. Alternatively, the procedure could be followed with non-literary genres such as recipes, newspaper articles, sets of instructions etc.
- Any other short story about old age, isolation, loneliness (Hemingway, *A Clean, Well-Lighted Place*; Joyce, *Clay*, etc.) could be used and the theme and how the topic is portrayed in the text could be explored more fully.
- Some suggestions of possible other texts and topics:
  Romantic love (Sir Walter Scott, *Lochinvar*, *Bonnie and Clyde*, pop ballads etc.)
  Relationships: Men vs. Women (Hemingway, *Hills like White Elephants, Cat in the Rain, A Very Short Story*)

Additional information on the texts

W. H. Auden, *Miss Gee* (1937)
Auden's ballad was often criticized for the discrepancy between the casual style and the gravity of the subject, and, in particular, for the cruelty of the last stanzas in which Miss Gee is dissected like an animal. Auden criticism likes to point out that the poet is trying to make us aware of our own cruelty and lack of respect for people like Miss Gee by making the reader first join in the laughter/derision of the old spinster and then feel all the more guilty when reading about her fate in the final stanzas.
T. Capote, *Miriam* (1945)
Capote's story is full of symbolic meanings and leaves ample room for discussion. When widowed Mrs H. T. Miller's isolation reaches a climax and she loses her sense of reality, her younger self, Miriam, intrudes in her life reminding her that she is more than the widow of late H. T. Miller and has a personality and a name of her own. Whether we read her psychological breakdown in the end as death, depends on how we interpret the symbols in the text.

5. Annotated bibliography

Bassnett, S. and P. Grundy (1995). *Language through Literature: Creative Language Teaching through Literature.* London: Longman.
A practical handbook using literature to improve students' language skills employing a range of imaginative techniques and providing originals ideas and creative activities.

Carter, R. A., and M. N. Long (1992). *Teaching Literature.* London: Longman.
A collection of useful activities and teaching techniques designed to raise students' interest in literature for both beginners and advanced students.

Collie, J. and S. Slater (1995*). Literature in the Language Classroom: A Resource Book of Ideas and Activities.* Cambridge: Cambridge University Press.
A practical guide for integrating literature work with language teach-

ing, offering a rationale and techniques for working with complete texts from all genres, including novels, short stories, plays and poems.

Lazar, G. (1993). *Literature and Language Teaching*. Cambridge: Cambridge University Press.

A practical guide with suggestions on how to teach literature in the language classroom and numerous tasks for immediate use in the classroom.

Rotter, W. and H. Bendl (1997/1999). *Your Companion to English Literary Texts*. Vol 1: *Analysis and Interpretation of Narrative Prose*; Vol. 2: *Analysis and Interpretation of Poetry and Drama*. Munich: Manz.

A very readable introduction to literary analysis providing all the necessary terminology, useful phrases and well-structured tables/diagrams and surveys.

Webliography

Savvidou, C. (2004). http://iteslj.org/Techniques/Savvidou-Literature.html [accessed 19.12.08]

A short article arguing in favour of using literature in the language classroom and offering practical suggestions on how this can be successfully achieved.

5.2. Popular Songs: Text in(to) Song – Song in(to) Text

Martina Elicker

1. Rationale

Songs, particularly popular song lyrics, can be used effectively in the advanced English language classroom for a wide range of language learning purposes, such as for awareness-raising in terms of register and style, focusing on particular aspects of grammar and syntax, and specific vocabulary work. Songs may also be used as the basis of text comparison activities (e.g., comparing different genres) and for free text production tasks. Popular song lyrics are a versatile text type which offers great potential for rich language work, and, above all, it is one which learners find motivating and fun to work with.

In this chapter, we will explore ways of exploiting Bob Dylan's 1975 song *Hurricane* for genre awareness purposes and in terms of register and style (spoken vs. written; formal vs. informal). Additionally, a newspaper article on the same topic (the real-life story of Rubin 'Hurricane' Carter, a US middleweight boxer who was tried and sentenced for triple murder in 1966) will be provided to illustrate the potential for genre comparison. These activities use the narrative genres and examine their forms across different text types and communicative contexts.

2. Procedure

(1) In pairs, students begin by re-telling each other their favourite story from a book or a film.
(2) They then consider what the characteristic features of a narrative are. Two questions may be used as prompts (see example materials 1). As many learners at this level are often familiar with the basic features of narratives, it may not be necessary to provide any additional input at this stage but simply elicit responses.
(3) Listening Comprehension: Students listen to a song which is in the form of a narrative, in this case the Bob Dylan song *Hurricane* (see

example materials 5 for lyrics). They should take notes in response to the characteristics elicited in stage 2. Alternatively, they may wish to find answers to the six classic questions which can be put on the board: who, what, where, when, why and how.

(4) Students get together in pairs and compare their notes, attempting to reconstruct the story in the song orally.

(5) Students are then asked to create a time-line chronology of events reported on in the song (see example materials 2). Students have to fill in the characters in the story and what they were doing at various points in time. This visual representation of the chronological structure of a narrative will help the learners to construct and sequence linear narratives in various forms later on. Attention will need to be paid to tenses in particular when working on these time-lines.

(6) Next students are provided with a text from a different genre, ideally, on the same topic. News reports are particularly well-suited to working on narrative structure. In the case of *Hurricane*, a news report on the same topic is available (see example materials 5). Students read the text and with their partner complete the same form of narrative content analysis as in stage 3.

(7) Students now also compare the two sets of responses. Whilst both texts are narratives and deal fundamentally with the same topic, it can be expected that they differ in some respects given the different text types and communicative contexts. Students then complete a table to mark the ways in which both text types are similar and different (see example materials 3).

(8) The teacher then elicits responses from the whole group on the tables they have completed. Guided by the teacher, the whole class discusses the core elements of narrative that remain across text types and also consider differences in specific characteristics of the two text types.

(9) Finally, the activity is transferred to the oral medium. Learners retell the stories from the original texts (song and/or news report) in pairs by taking on roles e.g., one is a journalist, one is a character from the story, one is a police officer, one is a witness etc.

(10) Students then consider the table used in stage 7 again in respect to how the oral dimension of narrative story-telling is similar or different to the song and the news report.

(11) The teacher can elicit responses to consider the nature of oral storytelling compared to the other narratives examined so far. (See example materials 4 for possible discussion questions).
(12) Finally, students can choose to write their own narratives in different genres, maintaining the core elements of a narrative structure and content, but adhering to the genre conventions they have identified.

3. Example materials

(1) Questions about narrative and possible responses in italics:

- What were the core components common to the stories you and your partner shared with each other?
  (Characters, time development, setting, problem, climax, ending)
- How did you and your partner structure your stories in terms of sequence of events?
  (Setting the scene, introduction of problem/catalyst, further stages of development, possible additional problems/catalysts, problem is solved, resolution/ending).

(2) Timeline table:

Under each area of the timeline below, fill in the character's name and what they were doing or what happened to them at that point:

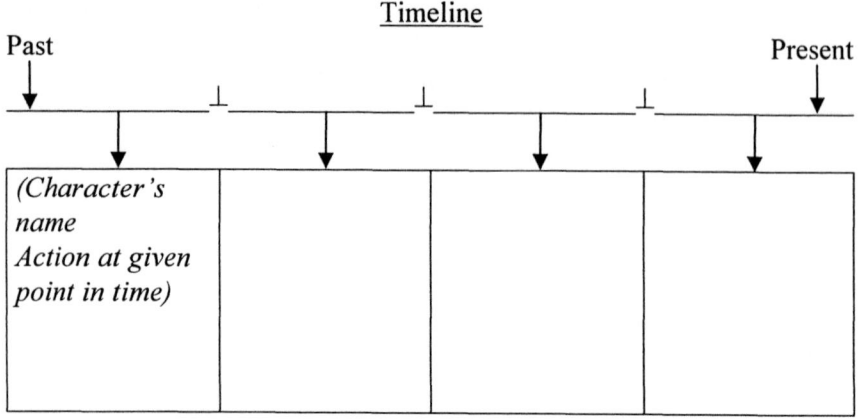

(3) Table to compare genres:

With a partner, you should consider the way in which the two genres are similar and different in respect to the following criteria:

	Similarities	**Differences**
Content		
Perspective		
Opinion/attitude		
Sequence of events		
Linguistic features		
Other		

(4) Possible discussion question for oral narratives:

- How linear was the structure of the oral story? Why was this? How are sequence and structure affected by the oral mode of storytelling?
- What non-linguistic cues were used to tell the story? How does this compare to written story telling? Which makes for easier/more interesting storytelling? Why?
- How does language and expression used vary across written and spoken? Can you give examples?

(5) Example song and news report:

> **Song: *Hurricane* by Bob Dylan**
>
> *Pistol shots ring out* in the barroom night
> Enter Patty Valentine from the upper hall.
> She sees the bartender in *a pool of blood*,
> Cries out, "My God, they *killed* them all!"
> Here comes the story of the Hurricane,
> The man the authorities came to *blame*
> *For* somethin' that he never done.
> *Put in a prison cell*, but one time he could-a been
> The champion of the world.
>
> *Three bodies lyin' there* does Patty see
> And another man named Bello, movin' around mysteriously.
> "I didn't do it," he says, and *he throws up his hands*
> "*I was only robbin' the register*, I hope you understand.
> I saw them leavin'," he says, and he stops
> "One of us had better *call up the cops*."
> And so Patty *calls the cops*
> And *they arrive on the scene with their red lights flashin'*
> In the hot New Jersey night.
>
> Meanwhile, far away in another part of town
> Rubin Carter and a couple of friends are drivin' around.
> Number one contender for the middleweight crown
> Had no idea what kinda shit was about to go down
> When *a cop pulled him over to the side of the road*
> Just like the time before and the time before that.
> In Paterson that's just the way things go.
> If you're black you might as well not show up on the street
> 'Less you wanna draw the heat.
>
> Alfred Bello had a partner and *he had a rap for the cops*.
> Him and Arthur Dexter Bradley were just out prowlin' around
> He said, "I saw two men runnin' out, they looked like middleweights
> They jumped into a white car with out-of-state plates."

And Miss Patty Valentine just nodded her head.
Cop said, "Wait a minute, boys, this one's not dead"
So they took him to the infirmary
And though this man could hardly see
They told him that *he could identify the guilty men.*

Four in the mornin' and they haul Rubin in,
Take him to the hospital and they bring him upstairs.
The wounded man looks up through his one dyin' eye
Says, "Wha'd you bring him in here for? He ain't the guy!"
Yes, here's the story of the Hurricane,
The man the authorities came to blame
For somethin' that he never done.
Put in a prison cell, but one time he could-a been
The champion of the world.

Four months later, the ghettos are in flame,
Rubin's in South America, fightin' for his name
While Arthur Dexter *Bradley's still in the robbery game*
And *the cops are puttin' the screws to him, lookin' for somebody to blame.*
"Remember that *murder* that happened in a bar?"
"Remember you said you saw *the getaway car*?"
"You think you'd like *to play ball with the law*?"
"Think it might-a been that fighter that you saw runnin' that night?"
"Don't forget that you are white."

Arthur Dexter Bradley said, "I'm really not sure."
Cops said, "A poor boy like you could use a break
We got you for the motel job and we're talkin' to your friend Bello
Now you don't wanta have to *go back to jail*, be a nice fellow.
You'll be doin' society a favor.
That sonofabitch is brave and getting' braver.
We want to put his ass in stir
We want to pin this triple murder on him
He ain't no Gentleman Jim."

Rubin could take a man out with just one punch
But he never did like to talk about it all that much.
It's my work, he'd say, and I do it for pay
And when it's over I'd just as soon go on my way
Up to some paradise
Where the trout streams flow and the air is nice
And ride a horse along a trail.
But then *they took him to the jailhouse*
Where they try to turn a man into a mouse.

All of Rubin's cards were marked in advance
The *trial* was a pig-circus, he never had a chance.
The *judge* made Rubin's *witnesses* drunkards from the slums
To the white folks who watched he was a revolutionary bum
And to the black folks he was just a crazy nigger.
No one doubted that *he pulled the trigger*.
And though *they could not produce the gun*,
The *D.A.* said he was the one who *did the deed*
And *the all-white jury agreed*.

Rubin Carter *was falsely tried*.
The *crime was murder "one,"* guess who *testified*?
Bello and Bradley and *they both baldly lied*
And the newspapers, they all went along for the ride.
How can the life of such a man
Be in the palm of some fool's hand?
To see him obviously framed
Couldn't help but make me feel ashamed to live in a land
Where *justice* is a game.

Now all the *criminals* in their coats and their ties
Are free to drink martinis and watch the sun rise
While Rubin sits like Buddha in *a ten-foot cell*
An innocent man in a living hell.
That's the story of the Hurricane,
But it won't be over till *they clear his name*
And give him back *the time he's done*.

Put in a prison cell, but one time he could-a been
The champion of the world.

(Bob Dylan / Jacques Levy 1975; [italics mine])
http://www.bobdylan.com/#/songs/hurricane-bob-dylan-and-jacques-levy [accessed 29.12.08]

News report:
Supreme Court Refuses to Revive Hurricane Carter's Murder Case
By SELWYN RAAB
Published: January 12, 1988

LEAD: <u>The United States Supreme Court</u> refused yesterday to consider *reinstating the triple-murder convictions of Rubin (Hurricane) Carter and John Artis*. It was the latest and perhaps the last chapter in a tangled 21-year *legal struggle*.

Mr. Carter, a onetime contender for the middleweight boxing championship, *was convicted in two trials and spent nearly 19 years in prison before his release in 1985*. In the mid-1970's, *before his second trial*, his *case* became a national cause celebre, with numerous civil rights leaders, politicians and entertainers speaking out for him.

Concerts to raise money for Mr. Carter were held in Madison Square Garden and in the Astrodome in Houston. Bob Dylan recorded a popular ballad, "Hurricane," which declared that Mr. Carter *had been framed by the police*. But the outcry of support for him largely subsided after Mr. Carter *was convicted a second time*, in 1976.

In their *ruling* yesterday, the <u>Supreme Court Justices</u> *denied a request* from New Jersey <u>prosecutors</u> to *review the case*. Without comment, they *let stand rulings* by <u>lower Federal courts</u> that Mr. Carter and Mr. Artis *had been unjustly convicted* because the Passaic County <u>Prosecutor's office</u> *suppressed critical evidence about a lie-detector test taken by a major prosecution witness*.

Both Mr. Carter and Mr. Artis *were convicted by juries* in 1967 and 1976, but *the verdicts were reversed* each time by <u>appeals courts</u> on the ground that *the constitutional rights of the defendants had been violated at each trial*.

The <u>Acting Passaic County Prosecutor</u>, John P. Goceljak, said yesterday that it was unclear if his office would *seek a third trial on murder charges*. Mr. Goceljak, in an interview, said he would consult with aides to the <u>New Jersey Attorney General</u>, W. Cary Edwards, before reaching a decision, probably within two weeks.

But <u>legal experts</u> said yesterday that a *new trial* would be unlikely.

Mr. Carter, in *a statement issued by his* <u>chief lawyer</u>, Myron Beldock, said, "I am exhilarated by the <u>court's decision</u> and relieved that this nightmare seems finally to be ending."

Mr. Carter *was arrested* in 1966 with Mr. Artis. They *were charged with the fatal shootings* of two men and a woman in the Lafayette Bar and Grill in Paterson, N.J.

Allegation of Racism

Mr. Carter and Mr. Artis, who are black, asserted that *the second trial was tainted by racism when the* <u>prosecution</u> introduced a theory that the Lafayette Grill victims, all of whom were white, *had been killed in revenge for the murder of a black tavern owner* in Paterson earlier that night.

In two decades of *courtroom conflicts*, Mr. Carter and Mr. Artis have steadfastly *maintained their innocence* and *presented alibi witnesses at both trials*. They contended that *evidence against them had been planted by detectives* and that <u>authorities</u> who were under pressure to *solve a major homicide case pressured witnesses to testify falsely*.

Mr. Carter, who is 50 years old, *was freed without bail* in November 1985, when a <u>Federal District Court judge</u> overturned the 1976 verdict.

Mr. Artis, who is 41, *served nearly 15 years on the murder charges before he was paroled* in 1981.

A *Cocaine Charge*

In June, Mr. Artis *pleaded guilty* in Passaic County *to conspiracy to distribute $50 worth of coca*ine and *to receiving a stolen handgun*. He *was sentenced to up to six years in prison*.

Lawyers for Mr. Artis *have appealed for a reconsideration of that sentence*, maintaining that it was *unduly harsh*. A lawyer for Mr. Artis, Lewis M. Steel, said yesterday that a Passaic County judge *wrongly cited Mr. Artis's involvement in the triple-murder case as a factor for a prison term*, instead of *granting him probation as a first offender*.

The *slayings* at the Lafayette Grill occurred at about 2:30 A.M. on June 17, 1966. Mr. Carter and Mr. Artis, who said they were casual acquaintances at the time, were picked up shortly after the *murders*. They were stopped because they were in a white car that resembled a vehicle in which *two gunmen had fled*.

Both men *were convicted* in May 1976, *largely on the testimony of* Alfred P. Bello and Arthur D. Bradley. Mr. Bello and Mr. Bradley *testified* that while *committing a burglary* near the Lafayette Grill, they had seen Mr. Carter, with a *shotgun*, and Mr. Artis, with a *handgun*, emerge from the grill.

Overturned in 1976

The convictions were overturned unanimously by the New Jersey Supreme Court in 1976 after Mr. Bello and Mr. Bradley independently *recanted their identifications*. Both *witnesses* said they *had been pressured by* detectives *to incriminate falsely* Mr. Carter and Mr. Artis *in return for favors in their own criminal cases*.

But at the *second trial* in 1976 Mr. Bello *reversed his recantation* and *again identified Mr. Carter and Mr. Artis as the gunmen*. Mr. Bradley *did not testify*.

Lie-Detector Test

In *appealing the second verdict*, defense lawyers argued *that the findings of a lie-detector test given to Mr. Bello shortly before the trial had been misrepresented to them*. According to the defense, findings that *impeached Mr. Bello's courtroom testimony* and showed that he *had been manipulated by* detectives and prosecutors *had been withheld from them*.

The New Jersey Supreme Court, in *a 4-to-3 ruling, upheld the second conviction* in 1982.

Defense lawyers said a shortage of funds delayed the *research and investigations* needed for the *appeal* and it took nine years to reach the Federal courts.

In November 1985, Judge Lee H. Sarokin in Federal District Court in Newark, citing *"grave constitutional violations"* by prosecutors, *dismissed the guilty verdicts.* Judge Sarokin *ruled that the* prosecution *had misstated the lie-detector findings* and *concealed evidence that might have led to acquittals.*

Judge Sarokin also *found* that Burrell I. Humphreys, who was the Passaic County Prosecutor in 1976 and who *personally tried the case,* had "fatally infected the trial" by suggesting, *without evidence,* to the *jury* that Mr. Carter and Mr. Artis *had committed the murders for racial revenge.*

*Ruling Uphe*ld

Judge Sarokin's 1985 *ruling was upheld unanimously* last August by the United States Court of Appeals for the Third Circuit in Philadelphia.

In a petition for permission to argue for reinstatement of the convictions before the Supreme Court, the prosecution said the *lie-detector findings would not have affected the outcome of the trial.*

Approval from four Justices *is required for the* Supreme Court *to hear a case.*

Leon Friedman, a professor at Hofstra University Law School, who was the lead appeals counsel for the defense, said in *a court brief* that the prosecution had asserted that the Federal courts should have *no right to rule on the importance of evidence, only on questions of law.*

Adoption of the prosecution's position, Mr. Friedman added, "would amount to a fundamental ousting of the historic responsibility of the Federal courts to *define the scope of constitutional error.*"

'Not Our Decision'

Mr. Beldock, a New York lawyer who *has represented* Mr. Carter for 13 years, said, "It is very difficult to conceive of *a third trial,* but it is not our decision."

Lawyers who have followed the *case* said it would be difficult *to try the case again* because the prosecution would have to rely on Mr. Bello, the sole witness who placed Mr. Carter and Mr. Artis at the murder scene. At two *trials, a recantation hearing and before a special grand jury*, Mr. Bello has provided three different versions of what happened *on the murder night*.

At *a hearing* in 1981 Mr. Bello, who *has been convicted of burglary and petty crimes*, acknowledged that he had been treated for alcoholism and emotional problems before the *second trial*. In 1981 he said he was living in Albuquerque, N.M., but Passaic County authorities declined to say yesterday if they knew his current whereabouts.

Judge Sarokin, in *dismissing the charges* in 1985, said that "even at its strongest links," the prosecution's "*chain of evidence had been substantially called into question by the petitioners.*"

Divorced While in Prison

During his *imprisonment*, Mr. Carter, who grew up in Paterson, *was divorced by his wife*, the mother of his two children.

Mr. Artis was married while *in prison* and returned to live in Paterson and to work at odd jobs. While in prison he was diagnosed as suffering from an incurable circulatory ailment, known as Buerger's Disease.

In an effort to halt the spread of the disease, Mr. Artis said, parts of five toes and two fingers have been amputated. In an interview, he said that he had used cocaine to soften the pain from his disease and in the hope that it might halt the infection.

He *denied ever selling cocaine* but said he had delivered a $50 package of the drug as a favor to his supplier.

(www.nytimes.com [italics and underlined expressions mine])[1]
http://query.nytimes.com/gst/fullpage.html?res=940DE6DC1E3EF931A25752C0A96E948260 [accessed: 19.12.08].

---

1 Italics represent legal terms and phrases, underlined expressions refer to terms used for legal professions and courts. See also possible variations for ESP (Legal English) activities.

4. Possible variations

The focus of the activities described above is on a more macro-level but there are also more linguistic, micro-level tasks that could be explored using songs. Some examples include:

- Gap-fills focusing on specific vocabulary (semantic fields etc – *Hurricane* is especially well-suited to work on legal English)
- Gap-fills focusing on grammatical features (e.g., verb forms, prepositions etc)
- Gap-fills focusing on style features (e.g., contractions, slang, idioms etc)

This song and the news report have been employed successfully in a legal English course. Some possible additional activities with this ESP focus are proposed below:

- Learners can describe the step-by-step development of the criminal case and characterize the parties involved. They can describe the crime scene in detail. They can describe the actual trial and its main aspects. Care will also need to be taken with specialist legal English for the US context, e.g., D.A. (i.e., district attorney) and "murder one" (i.e., murder in the first degree).
- Divide the class into two groups: one group can prepare arguments for, the other against the defendant's case. Then organize the students into groups of four (2 students for and 2 students against) and have them defend their positions in a 10-minute discussion (emphasis on General English language skills such as arguing, agreeing, disagreeing).
- Students can act out the initial stage of the trial. Students are divided into three groups: one group prepares the opening statement for the prosecution, the second for the defense; the remaining students are assigned different roles (e.g., judge, bailiff, defendant) and given any language help required in order to prepare for their roles. Subsequently the students act out the scene in groups (focus on in-court language use, steps in a trial).
- A simulation of the in-court proceedings of the entire case can be done.

- As a register transfer task, ask the students to rewrite the song in more formal English. Learners should first analyze typical informal linguistic elements in the song, e.g., phonetic representations such as *wanna*, and the omission of -ing endings as in *fightin'* and *somethin'* to slang expressions such as *sonofabitch* and *what kinda shit*.
- A lexical task for legal English could be to try to find all the terms relating to legal professions, legal proceedings (e.g., persons involved in a trial), crimes and punishment. Learners could also discuss the courts mentioned in the text and how they fit within the US court system. Another task could be to create word families based on key words such as murder, law, deny, convict, innocence.

5. Annotated bibliography

Harris, M. A. (1997). *Legal Writing. Principles of Juriography*. Upper Saddle River, NJ.: Prentice Hall.
A practical introduction to the basics of legal writing.

Hoey, M. (2001). *Textual Interaction: An Introduction to Written Discourse Analysis*. London: Routledge.
Hoey offers an original matrix perspective on text structure using time bands.

Murphey, T. (1992). *Music & Song*. Oxford: Oxford University Press.
A practical book providing a wide variety of ideas of how songs can be used in the EFL classroom.

Webliography

Deal, Cal "Hurricane Carter: The Other Side of the Story"
http://www.graphicwitness.com/carter/song.html [accessed 26.08.08].

Raab, S. (1988). "Supreme Court Refuses to Revive Hurricane Carter's Murder Case", *New York Times*. January 12, 1988. http://www.nytimes.com
http://query.nytimes.com/gst/fullpage.html?res=940DE6DC1E3EF931A25752C0A96E948260 [accessed 19.12.98]

"The Case Against Carter: Prosecutor's Response to Judge Sarokin's Decision"

http://www.graphicwitness.com/carter/sarokinresponse.html#carID [accessed 26.08.08]
http://en.wikipedia.org/wiki/Bob_Dylan [accessed 16.12.08]
http://www.bobdylan.com/#/songs [accessed 16.12.08] (Bob Dylan lyrics)
http://www.youtube.com/watch?v=Ei0yDMFVaRs [accessed 26.08.08] (Bob Dylan performing 'Hurricane').
Schoepp, K. (2001) Reasons for using songs in the EFL/ESL classroom. http://iteslj.org/Articles/Schoepp-Songs.html [accessed 16.12.08] (Article discussing reasons for using songs in the EFL classroom)

Other media

Dylan, B. (1976). "Hurricane", *Desire*. Columbia Records.

5.3. Transferring Content across Genres

Sarah Mercer and Jennifer Schumm

1. Rationale

The authors have observed that many students still need considerable support and structure when writing at tertiary level. Very often they have differing expectations of text conventions from their culture to the target culture and lack the confidence to write freely in their L2. In particular, students can find it difficult to use appropriate language, select relevant content, structure and layout texts according to genre conventions that are culturally appropriate for their L2. In order to be able to communicate effectively in writing, the authors feel that an understanding of genre is essential and can help address many of these difficulties.

A metacognitive awareness of linguistic and structural characteristics of various text types facilitates student writing in different contexts. By discussing and sensitising students to various text conventions and the communicative purpose of different text types, learners develop the skills to write in a culturally and linguistically appropriate manner. Whilst the authors are conscious of variation within individual genres and are cautious about not being overly prescriptive, they have found that scaffolding learners' writing experiences by using genre frameworks and a structured approach at the outset of writing programmes at tertiary level appears to help learners to develop more confidence to write freely in English. With an increased awareness of the role of genre expectations in effective written communication, learners are able to move towards text production in genres that are less predictable in terms of their conventions and typical characteristics.

2. Procedure

(1) Students are given a narrative text to read (see example materials 1). The story should follow a linear chronological sequence of events and involve the typical characteristics of a narrative, e.g., characters,

setting, atmosphere, climax, etc. A narrative is selected for two main reasons: firstly its simplicity and secondly for its familiarity to students from many cultural backgrounds.

(2) In pairs, students complete a chart outlining the main narrative characteristics which occur in the text (see example materials 2).

(3) The teacher displays an incomplete chart on an OHP and elicits responses from the student pairs so that the whole class completes the chart together.

(4) Students remain working in pairs and are presented with a collection of 3 recipes (see example materials 3). They are asked to analyse the recipes in terms of typical genre features (see example materials 4). Depending on the level and needs of the learners, the range and amount of genre variation can be varied.

(5) Next, students get together with another pair to compare their answers and together the 4 students draw up a list of the key characteristics of a recipe in terms of the criteria outlined in the chart – layout, content, linguistics features etc.

(6) Using the recipe genre as a basis and impulse for discussion, the whole class discusses the concept of genre generally (see example materials 5 for possible discussion questions about the nature of genre).

(7) Once the teacher feels confident that the students have understood the typical characteristics of the recipe genre, the students are asked in pairs to transfer the content from the narrative using their charts completed in steps 2 and 3 to the form of a recipe (see example materials 6). They should also invent a title for their recipe.

(8) When the students have completed their texts, they stick them up on the walls around the classroom together with a feedback sheet. The other students walk round and read the texts. If they feel genre conventions have not been adhered to, then they make a note of which part and why on the attached feedback sheet.

3. Example materials

(1) Model Email Anecdote

> Hi Julie!
> How's things going? Things have been crazy around here. Actually, I've just got back from a trip to Vienna with Peter. You know the guy who you met at the start-of-term party with the green spiky hair? Well, you'll never believe what happened to us – it'll blow your mind!
>
> Anyway, the journey out there was totally uneventful, but once we got off the train in Vienna, our trip took a turn for the worse. It all started when I wanted to buy tram tickets. As usual, I had my green backpack with all the badges on it with me but when I looked in my bag, I realised I had the most enormous hole at the bottom and my purse must've dropped out somewhere along the way. What a nightmare! Bad luck, you might say, could have happened to anyone. But read on!
>
> After racing around the whole station and harassing all the staff there, we finally had to admit defeat and accept the purse was lost for good. We tried to see the bright side of things. Thankfully, Peter still had his money with him and, to my delight, my camera hadn't fallen out. But what happened next really dampened our spirits.
>
> So, we got to my favourite square in Vienna – Stefansplatz – and stopped this guy who looked perfectly respectable to ask him to take our piccie. No sooner had we handed him our camera, than he sprinted off down the main street and ducked off into a dark alley. We couldn't believe our eyes! Could things possibly get any worse?
>
> Yes – they could! In all of the excitement, Peter hadn't realised that someone had pick-pocketed him and lifted his wallet. We were now stranded in Vienna with not a penny to our names, and it was only 10am in the morning – what were we going to do for the rest of the day? Things seemed so grim that we didn't know what else to do but laugh uncontrollably.
>
> And to top it all, at that moment, it started to come down in buckets, and, of course, we didn't have any raingear with us! Typical! Luckily, we still had the return part of our train ticket but just needed to make our way back to the station. So, we trudged through the rain

soaked to the skin and dropped onto the return train with a huge sigh of relief!

What a disaster of a day from start to finish! As you can imagine, we're not going back to Vienna in a hurry! So, is there a moral to this story you might ask? Well, they say troubled times bring people closer together, and, on that day, I found out what a great guy Peter is and how well we get on – in spite of everything! So, maybe the day wasn't so bad after all. I'll let you know what happens with us!

Hope all is well with you and that your exam went ok – I'm sure you aced it! Drop me a line when you've got time.
Bye for now,
Anna

(2) Chart for narrative characteristics of the email story:

Characters
Setting
Mood & atmosphere
Sequence of events

(3) Recipes taken from: http://www.recipesource.com/ [accessed 2.12.2008].

Austrian Homestyle Generic Soup

Serves: 3

Amount	Measure	Ingredients
4	tb	Butter or margarine (or oil, – or lard)
3	tb	All purpose flour
1 1/2	pt	Water
3 1/2	ts	Beef Flavor Consomme
2	tb	Chopped onion
1	md	Carrot, diced
2	c	(approx.) broccoli or – cauliflower, cut into small pieces
1	md	Potato, peeled and diced

Melt butter over medium heat. Add flour, stirring constantly, until the mixture becomes puffy. Add water, bouillon powder, onions, potatoes and carrots. Bring to a boil, stirring occasionally. Reduce heat and simmer until potatoes are almost done (about 5 to 6 minutes). Add broccoli and return to boil. Simmer for another minute.

Makes 3 large servings (which with a chunk of French bread or the like would make a hearty meal, quantity-wise.)

Double Chocolate Fudgey Brownies with Walnuts

Serves: 1

Amount	Measure	Ingredients
4	squares	unsweetened chocolate
3/4	cup	unsalted butter
1 3/4	cups	sugar
3		eggs

1	cup	flour
1	teaspoon	vanilla
1	cup	walnuts – chopped
1	cup	semisweet chocolate chips

Preheat oven to 325 degrees Fahrenheit.

Line a 13" x 9" glass pan with a double layer of tin foil. Extend the foil ends a couple of inches over the shorter side of the pan. Grease the tin foil with butter.

In a large microwave proof bowl, place unsweetened chocolate and butter. Heat until melted, about 3 minutes or so. Mix in sugar, blend well. Allow to cool a little. Add the three eggs; beat in well. Now add the flour, blending it in well. Add the nuts.

Pour batter into the prepared baking dish. Sprinkle the chocolate chips evenly over the batter.

Bake at 325 degrees for 30 minutes or until a toothpick comes out clean. Don't overcook this. Remove from oven. Allow to cool before cutting.

Cut into portions which meet with your discretion! Should make around 20. This is a dense, chewy, fudgey type brownie.

Broccoli Mushroom Casserole

Serves: 4

Amount	Measure	Ingredients
1 1/2	lb	Broccoli
6	tb	Butter or margarine
1/4	c	Flour
1/2	ts	Salt
1/4	ts	Black pepper
2	c	Milk
1	c	Shredded cheddar cheese

1/2	lb	Small mushrooms
2	tb	Chopped green bell pepper
		Additional shredded cheese
		i. (optional)
		Paprika

Separate broccoli stalks and cook in 1 inch boiling salted water 3 to 5 minutes. Drain. Arrange broccoli in greased 9-inch square pan. Melt 5 tablespoons butter and blend in flour, salt and pepper. Cook and stir until smooth. Remove from heat and stir in milk. Bring to boil and boil 1 minute, stirring constantly. Add cheese and remove from heat. Sauté mushrooms in remaining 1 tablespoon butter until tender and add to sauce. Add green pepper and cook 1 minute. Pour sauce over broccoli. Sprinkle with additional cheese and paprika, if desired.

Bake at 350F 15 to 20 minutes.

Serves 4 generously and is delicious with crusty bread.

(4) Chart for analysing recipe genre including examples of possible answers in italics:

Genre Characteristics of a Recipe
Layout:
List of ingredients
Instructions sequenced in steps
Content:
Ingredients
Oven temperatures if necessary
Timing
Utensils
Measurements
Stages of preparation and cooking processes
Possible variations
Possible commentary by author

Examples from specific semantic field:
Cup, teaspoons, oven, temperature, bake, stir, mix, sprinkle, combine, puree, cut etc,
Language features:
Imperative forms of the verb   *Missing articles*   *Sequence markers*   *Short, concise sentences*   *Abbreviations*

(5) Possible discussion questions about the nature of genre:

a. What are the characteristics of the genre 'recipe'?
b. How do you recognise different genres? (e.g., a diary entry, a magazine article, a newspaper report, an academic paper etc)
c. Why do you think an understanding of genre is important?
d. In what ways is an understanding of genre important for appropriate register use?
e. What lessons have you learnt from this session about your own writing?
f. What specific questions will you ask yourself in future when asked to write in a particular genre?

(6) Example of possible recipe text based on email in example materials 1.

Recipe for a disastrous day in Vienna, Austria
Serves: 2
Amount   Measure   Ingredients   ----------   ------------   -------------------------------   2 round trip   tickets to Vienna from city/town of choice   1 large size   hole at the bottom of your backpack   2 normal size   wallets (one per person)

1 ounce	*trust in respectable-looking people*
1 unexpected	*encounter with a pickpocket*
1 ounce	*humour (add more if desired)*

Don't add any raingear to backpack with hole at bottom while preparing for day trip to Vienna.

Get on train to Vienna in the morning with backpack with hole at bottom. Get off train in Vienna – don't forget backpack – and buy tram tickets. Discover hole at bottom of backpack and missing wallet number 1. Run round train station looking for missing wallet. Accept situation and walk to Stefansplatz. Mix in a respectable-looking man. Ask man to take your picture. Watch as he runs away with your camera and ducks off into a dark alley. Add unexpected encounter with a pickpocket. Then notice wallet number 2 is missing. Mix in ounce of humour – you can add as much as desired. Prepare to walk back to train station. Don't forget to get caught in a rain storm without rain gear. Once at train station, get on train to city/town of morning departure. Swear never to go back to Vienna in near future.

If a particularly disastrous day is desired, get on train going in the opposite direction to the train to city/town of morning departure.

Serves 2 generously. Guarantees bad humour.

4. Possible variations

The activity suggested here uses a genre that is easy for introducing students to the concept of genre. However, the basic idea can be adapted to other genres and students could be asked to produce both texts, e.g., from a factual travel guide text into a tourist brochure or newspaper report into a personal email etc.

You may also wish to add a stage where students examine an example of a recipe that does not conform to genre. Students have to identify which aspects are not appropriate for the genre and re-write it so that it adheres to all genre conventions established in steps 4 and 5. In the example given below, problems with genre convention are:

1. No measurements given for the ingredients
2. No use of imperative verbs
3. Poorly marked sequencing
4. Wordy and vague

Macaroni & Cheese

Serves: 4
Preparation Time: 0:30

Ingredients:
Macaroni
Butter
Cream
Cheddar cheese
Worcestershire sauce

You should try to cook the macaroni until it feels as soft as you like to eat it. I like to drain it off and return it to the pot for a little more drying time. Most people I know melt butter and add some cream and cheese which they heat up together. This makes a delicious Macaroni and cheese, especially if you add some Worcestershire sauce to spice it up a little.

---

5. Annotated bibliography

Cory, H. (1999). *Advanced Writing with English in Use.* Oxford: Oxford University Press.
   A coursebook that addresses issues of genre and key areas of writing, especially register.
Hyland, K (2004). *Genre and Second Language Writing.* Michigan: The University of Michigan Press.
   An excellent introduction to some background and theory about writing and genre.
Paltridge, B. (2001). *Genre and the Language Learning Classroom.* Michigan: The University of Michigan Press.

A more practical guide to classroom activities and assessment procedures using the genre-based approach.

Swales, J. (1990). *Genre Analysis: English in Academic and Research Settings.* Cambridge: Cambridge University Press.

An essential book for an understanding of genre analysis and the teaching of writing and register awareness.

White, R. and V. Arndt (1991). *Process Writing.* Harlow: Longman.

A key practical work with many ideas to help scaffold students' awareness of writing processes.